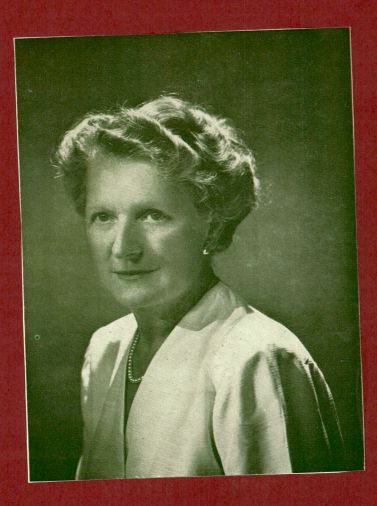

TWAYNE'S WORLD AUTHORS SERIES

A Survey of the World's Literature

Sylvia E. Bowman, Indiana University

GENERAL EDITOR

CANADA

Joseph Jones, University of Texas

EDITOR

Ethel Wilson

(TWAS 33)

TWAYNE'S WORLD AUTHORS SERIES (TWAS)

The purpose of TWAS is to survey the major writers—novelists, dramatists, historians, poets, philosophers, and critics—of the nations of the world. Among the national literatures covered are those of Australia, Canada, China, Eastern Europe, France, Germany, Greece, India, Italy, Japan, Latin America, New Zealand, Poland, Russia, Scandinavia, Spain, and the African nations, as well as Hebrew, Yiddish, and Latin Classical literatures. This survey is complemented by Twayne's United States Authors Series and English Authors Series.

The intent of each volume in these series is to present a critical-analytical study of the works of the writer; to include biographical and historical material that may be necessary for understanding, appreciation, and critical appraisal of the writer; and to present all material in clear, concise English—but not to vitiate the scholarly content of the work by doing so.

Ethel Wilson

By DESMOND PACEY

The University of New Brunswick

Twayne Publishers, Inc.   ::   New York

To
my wife
and
four daughters

MANUFACTURED IN THE UNITED STATES OF AMERICA

Preface

THIS book has the advantages and disadvantages of a pioneer study. Although Ethel Wilson has established a modest international reputation since her writings first began to appear in the late nineteen-thirties, surprisingly little critical attention has been paid to her work, and this is the first book-length study of it. As a result, I am denied that stimulation which comes from comparing one's own impressions and conclusions with those of other critics. On the other hand, there is a challenge in being the first to chart the development of a writer for whom one has an intense admiration.

Since this is the first full-dress critical study of Ethel Wilson, I have chosen to consider her work in the most straightforward and simple way: first of all by outlining her literary career and attempting to place her in the tradition of English fiction, then by analyzing her individual works in chronological order, and finally by making a tentative assessment of her contribution to the literature of Canada and the world.

I wish to express my gratitude to various people who have helped with this study, but who are not of course in any way responsible for its short-comings. My greatest thanks must go to Mrs. Wilson herself, who has written encouraging and informative letters to me over a period of almost twenty years. John Gray of the Macmillan Company of Canada was kind enough to lend me his personal copy of *Hetty Dorval* and to give me information about the sales and printings of Mrs. Wilson's books. Mrs. Janet Bjorn and Mrs. Charlotte Pitt typed most of the manuscript for me, and endured my bad hand-writing without complaint. Professors David Galloway and Lauriat Lane, my colleagues in the Department of English of the University of New Brunswick, and Mr. Robert Campbell, a graduate student in that

Department, helped with bibliographical details, and Dr. Lane kindly read the book in typescript. As always, my wife's patient encouragement was unfailing.

DESMOND PACEY

The University of New Brunswick

Acknowledgments

The passages from Mrs. Wilson's novels and short stories are quoted with the kind permission of her publishers, the Macmillan Company of Canada, the Macmillan Company of London, the Macmillan Company of New York, and Harper and Row, New York.

Contents

Chronology

1888   Ethel Wilson born on January 20 at Port Elizabeth, South Africa, daughter of Robert William Bryant and Lila (Malkin) Bryant.

1890   On death of her mother, taken by her father to England; cared for by maternal grandparents and aunts in Staffordshire.

1898   To Vancouver, British Columbia, on the death of her father. Lived with her grandmother, Mrs. James Malkin, an aunt, and a great aunt. Attended Miss Gordon's School (now Crofton House).

1902–
1906   At girls' boarding school, Trinity Hall School, Southport, in England. Passed London Matriculation.

1907   Graduated from Vancouver Normal School, Advanced Session. Received Second Class Teacher's Certificate.

1907–
1920   Taught in various Vancouver public schools; the Kitsilano Elementary (1907–1909), the Model School (1909–1912), the Lord Roberts School (1914–1918), Dawson Elementary (1918–1920).

1921   Jan. 4—married Dr. Wallace Wilson, who was to become a very distinguished Vancouver doctor and to serve as president of the Canadian Medical Association from 1946 to 1947. During the long, happy marriage Dr. and Mrs. Wilson travelled extensively in Canada, the Levant, southern Europe, Scandinavia, and England.

1930   Accompanied her husband to Vienna where he continued his specialist studies in internal medicine. En route the couple stopped off at Algiers, Egypt, Palestine, Turkey, Greece and Italy.

1937   First short story, "I Just Love Dogs," published on December 4 in *The New Statesman and Nation*.

1938 Visited England, her husband representing Canada at the annual meeting of the British Medical Association.

1940–
1945 Dr. Wallace Wilson served in the Canadian Army. Mrs. Wilson edited a Red Cross magazine in Vancouver.

1947 Publication of *Hetty Dorval*. Visit to Paris, where Dr. Wilson represented Canada at the first meeting of the World Health Organisation.

1949 Publication of *The Innocent Traveller*. Visited Portugal.

1952 Publication of *The Equations of Love*.

1954 Publication of *Swamp Angel*. Second visit to Portugal.

1955 Given honorary degree of D.Litt. by the University of British Columbia.

1956 Publication of *Love and Salt Water*.

1961 Publication of *Mrs. Golightly and Other Stories*. Awarded special medal by Canada Council for her contribution to Canadian Literature.

1964 Awarded Lorne Pierce Gold Medal by the Royal Society of Canada.

1966 March 12—death of Mrs. Wilson's husband, Dr. Wallace Wilson.

CHAPTER 1

Introduction

ETHEL Wilson is a writer of small output but of high quality. She has published only six short novels, eighteen short stories, and nine essays. She did not rush into print—she was forty-nine when she published her first story, fifty-nine when she published her first book—and she has never shown any eagerness for fame or commercial success. Upon everything that she writes is the mark of a fastidious and exigent craftsman: her art is quiet, gentle, controlled, exquisitely fashioned and finished.

Since all her books have appeared since the end of World War II, in the era of the angry young men and the beat generation, they may seem at first rather old-fashioned, and they have occasionally been so described by reviewers. If we remind ourselves, however, that she was born in 1888, and that as a person, if not as a writer, she was the approximate contemporary of E. M. Forster, James Joyce, Virginia Woolf, D. H. Lawrence, T. S. Eliot, Katherine Mansfield, and Aldous Huxley, we realize that she is not such a "sport" as we might otherwise conclude. As we shall point out more fully below, her work bears marked resemblances to that of some of these writers, especially Forster and Woolf. But even if she were a "sport," this would not at all disturb Mrs. Wilson: she has several times expressed her distaste for fashions in writing, and she has always gone her own way, indifferent to the fads of the day.

I *Her Manner*

Ethel Wilson is certainly not an experimental novelist in the usual sense of that phrase: she employs no tricks of chronology

or typography, makes little use of stream of consciousness, does
not introduce newspaper headlines nor often employ cinematic
techniques such as the flashback and montage. Her stories are
almost always told in straightforward chronological order by an
omniscient narrator, a narrator who is not above commenting
occasionally, in a very old-fashioned way, on the persons and
events he is narrating. But in the deeper and truer sense of the
phrase, Mrs. Wilson *is* an experimental novelist. In each story
that she writes, one feels that she has searched for and found
the most perfect means to express her unique vision, that she
has waited patiently for what she calls "an incandescence":

> There is a moment, I think, within a novelist of any orig-
> inality, whatever his country or his scope, when some sort
> of synthesis takes place over which he has only partial con-
> trol. There is an incandescence, and from it meaning emerges,
> words appear, they take shape in their order, a fusion occurs.
> A minor writer, whose gift is small and canvas limited,
> stands away at last if he can and regards what he has done,
> without indulgence. This is a counsel of perfection which
> I myself am not able to take with skill, but I must try to
> take it. I am sure that the very best writing in our country
> will result from such an incandescence which takes place
> in a prepared mind where forces meet.[1]

Because she is so resolutely independent in her search for
form, her work is difficult to classify. Certainly she is a novelist
rather than a romancer or an anatomist, but what kind of novelist?
One's first instinct might be to call her a novelist of manners,
since she has a remarkably sharp eye for the nuances of social
behaviour in a given place—usually Vancouver or other parts
of British Columbia—at a given time, the first half of the twentieth century. But on second thought one must conclude that
her interest is less in society than in individuals, and be inclined
to describe her as a novelist of character, or a psychological
realist. This is more accurate, but it is not really adequate:
memorable as the characters of her novels are, they are sometimes overshadowed by the theme, and this in turn would lead us
to describe her as a novelist of ideas. Even this is misleading,
for it suggests that her novels are like those, say, of Aldous
Huxley, in which the characters tend to be mere mouthpieces

of conflicting philosophies. Her characters are living individuals
in their own right, and the themes of her novels cannot be expressed in abstract terms. What she is ultimately concerned with
is the truth of the human condition on earth, presented not in
abstract generalizations but through sensuous particularity.

II   *Literary Preferences and Influences*

If it is difficult and indeed finally impossible to attach a neat
label to Ethel Wilson's fiction, it is easier to suggest the nature
of her work by defining its scope and pointing out her affiliations
to other writers. She is not in any sense a sensational writer.
There is a great deal of love, and some lust, in her stories, but
no "sex" in the sense of clinical descriptions of sexual activity.
It is clear from her references to the marital relationship that she
approves of, and indeed glories in, physical relations between
man and wife, but she does not consider it necessary to describe
the various postures of coitus or the details of foreplay. There
are acts of violence in her stories—murders, attempted suicides,
near-drownings—but they are usually passed over quickly, or take
place off-stage. Although there are very occasional political overtones—as, for example, in the short story "We have to sit opposite"—there is little concern for political issues and nothing
even approaching political partisanship or propaganda. Although
she shows herself aware of the debilitating effects of poverty,
there is nothing in her stories that could properly be described
as social protest. Nor does she express pessimism about the
human condition, aware as she is of human fragility in an immense and largely indifferent universe. On the other hand, there
is no strongly optimistic assertion, resulting from a transcendental
leap. Occasional references in her novels make it apparent that
she believes in God and in the efficacy of prayer, but the effective
basis of her view of life is her qualified confidence in the capacity
of men and women to endure. She blows no trumpets over man's
triumph; rather she quietly murmurs that as a species he will
somehow manage to survive.

The references to, and quotations from, other writers in the
work of Ethel Wilson suggest the breadth of her reading, the
eclecticism of her tastes, and her temperamental affinities. Among
the writers to whom she alludes with various degrees of approval

and admiration are Shakespeare, Donne, Henry James, Henry
Fielding, James Joyce, William Faulkner, Marcel Proust, Lewis
Carroll, Ivy Compton-Burnett, Herbert Read, E. M. Forster,
Somerset Maugham, Anatole France, Joseph Conrad, Jane Austen, Paul Verlaine, Alexander Pushkin, Edmund Waller, Brian
Moore, Joyce Cary, Anthony Trollope, Katherine Mansfield,
Colette, Daniel Defoe, Virginia Woolf, and Arnold Bennett. All
of these may well have influenced her in one way or another,
but it would be tedious and unprofitable to attempt to deal with
them all. Donne and Shakespeare often crop up in her work in
the form of thematic quotations, for example, and their influence
is probably a very general one. Some of the writers in the above
list, however, if they did not exactly "influence" her, were important in her development in the sense that they showed her
what the novel was capable of achieving.

In a letter dated July 12, 1953, Mrs. Wilson wrote:

> I am not conscious of being influenced by any writers, but
> am aware that my taste runs to economy in writing—with
> some glorious exceptions. Some of the novels I most love are
> *Tom Jones, Moll Flanders,* the matter-of-fact statement of
> *Roxana the Fortunate Mistress* (so much disliked by Ford
> Madox what's his name), three in particular of E. M. For-
> ster's novels, the first two or three volumes of Proust, much
> Trollope, one or two (but not en masse) of I. Compton-
> Burnett—and I would say that the limpid style of most of
> them, the lack of pretentiousness, the fact that these people
> have something to say, with skill, with good heart, often
> with deep feeling yet with some cynicism, their detachment
> as well as their involvement, gives one inexpressible pleasure.
> They have *style,* each his own, and without style . . . how
> dull.[2]

We must notice in passing the references there to economy,
matter-of-fact statement, limpid style, lack of pretentiousness,
and a combination of involvement and detachment, for all of
these are strong features of Ethel Wilson's own work. But for
the moment I am more interested in speculating why Mrs. Wilson
is attracted to these particular authors, and what bearing this
attraction has upon her own work.

She gives us one clue to her admiration for Defoe when she

speaks of the matter-of-factness of *Roxana*. She amplifies this in another letter:

> Yet, enormously as I admire her [Jane Austen] and her circumstantial accompaniments, I read the landing of Robinson Crusoe—the successive waves that throw him on the beach, the indisputable detail that seems irrelevant but isn't, the detail that shows that "this was so, and thus it happened," of Roxana or Moll, and *then* I catch the real fever of admiration.[3]

Defoe sticks doggedly to reality, and insists that his books are histories rather than romances. We continually get from his novels the sense that this was the way it actually happened, a feeling of immediate reality and truth. His devotion to detail, especially to physical and financial and social detail, is the chief source of this effect. Now this sense of reality is very strong also in the novels of Ethel Wilson. Although she is more impressionistic, more selective, than Defoe, we always feel that her stories are the products of sustained observation rather than of fantasy. Her characters are set firmly in a certain place at a certain time, and we see, for example, their kitchens and their living-rooms, their hats and their shoes, and learn their occupations and their recreations. Mrs. Wilson has written, "I cannot imagine willingly employing even a marginal character without knowing his outside appearance so well that he could be identified on the street by myself and for my own purposes."[4]

But the affinity with Defoe goes deeper than that. Defoe was especially interested in a certain kind of character—a person, usually a woman, who began life under severe handicaps and who somehow managed to survive and indeed to achieve a kind of triumph. Moll and Roxana achieved this by dubious, indeed by unsavoury, means, but for all their wiles and deceits we accord them a reluctant admiration. Now this kind of person interests Mrs. Wilson also: Lilly, of *Lilly's Story* in *The Equations of Love*, is just such a heroine, and Maggie Vardoe, of *Swamp Angel*, is another.

The affinity with Fielding's *Tom Jones* is more difficult to perceive. The rollicking robustness of Fielding's novel seems far removed from the quiet fidelity to ordinary life which marks most of Ethel Wilson's work. Humour, of course, is one link;

there is a great deal of humour in Ethel Wilson, especially in
The Innocent Traveller which might well be called, as Fielding
insisted on calling *Tom Jones,* a comic epic in prose. Fielding
and Ethel Wilson are both adept at the humour of character,
the humour of situation, and the more subtle humour of irony.
Fielding, with his distrust of religious enthusiasm, would have
delighted in the Reverend Elmer Pratt and the revivalist meeting
which he conducts in the "I have a Father in the Promised Land"
episode in *The Innocent Traveller.*

Another link between Fielding and Wilson is the basic affirmation of life which their work expresses. Both are yea-sayers,
who see the folly, hypocrisy, pettiness, cruelty and fragility
of man but yet declare that life is good and that people are
fundamentally worthy. They combine, in short, "deep feeling with
some cynicism."[5] Mrs. Wilson may lack Fielding's physical
robustness, but she has a similar toughness of spirit.

If Fielding seems rather too robust for Mrs. Wilson's taste,
Proust seems a little too etiolated and introverted, and it is a
sign of her tolerant eclecticism that she can praise them both.
What attracted her to Proust, I believe, is his patient reconstruc-
tion of the past. *The Innocent Traveller* is itself an attempt to
recover lost time, to bring back to life the daily routine of Mrs.
Wilson's grandparents, uncles and aunts, to savour once more
the flavour of past days. The tone—witty, light-hearted, healthily
ironic—is very different from Proust, but the method is similar,
since it relies so heavily upon the accumulation of detail and the
association of ideas.

The connection with E. M. Forster is more obvious. Forster's
wry humanism, his respect for the individual, his strong sense
of place, his gentle and humane liberalism, his respect for both
intelligence and emotional sensitivity, his enthusiasm for the
arts and his deep distrust of mere business efficiency are all
attitudes which Mrs. Wilson shares. Both often affect a comic
or at least light-hearted manner but are fundamentally concerned with the ultimate meaning of life, the relation of man to
the universe, the proper relationship between man and his fellow-
man, and the nature of "reality." Both are products of an English
upper-middle-class culture, respectful of its finest features and
anxious to perpetuate them, yet both are aware of the limitations
of that culture and of its vulnerability from both internal and

external enemies. Lionel Trilling has asserted that "the undeveloped heart" is the central theme of Forster's novels; as we shall
see, it could also be said to be the central theme of Mrs. Wilson's.
Forster and Wilson are both novelists in whose work a usually
quiet surface is occasionally disrupted by bursts of violence; and
they both combine intellectual detachment with moments of
visionary insight.

Ethel Wilson's affinity with Trollope and Ivy Compton-Burnett
lies in their shared concern with the family chronicle and the
combinations and permutations within the family relationship.
All three writers delight in the eccentricities of character, and
see the closed circle of the family as an ideal arena in which to
display the interplay of these eccentricities. There are only a
few traces in Ethel Wilson's work of the macabre and the ab-
normal which is so frequently found in Ivy Compton-Burnett;
in this respect she is closer to the gentle irony of Trollope.

When I received the above letter from Mrs. Wilson I was
struck by certain omissions from her list of affinities. From reading her work, I had expected her to mention Jane Austen and
Virginia Woolf among her admirations. When I questioned her
about this, she replied that she found Jane Austen pleasurable
but not truly exciting, Virginia Woolf too narrowly patrician.
Her reply also served to bring out another admiration which
should have occurred to me but had not—namely Arnold Bennett.
Here is a portion of that letter:

> Virginia Woolf.—An extremely feminine and narrow preju-
> dice reminds me as I read her that her view of life is
> patrician to the point, sometimes, of not understanding.
> Perhaps my memory plays me false—but it seemed to me
> that she mis-read entirely Arnold Bennett (not in his more
> florid novels) and his view of poor persons, poor houses,
> poor places, mean streets, and their relative beauty and
> importance to those concerned—both dwellers and observers.
> She was surprisingly blind to all that. She was very noble in
> character, enormously gifted, fascinating, I think. I cannot
> maintain interest in the longer books although she has a
> heavenly pen. *To the Lighthouse* is written with a heavenly
> pen. . . . Her death combines with her life, her friendships,
> her writing, to make her very distinguished. I re-read her,

but can refrain. But yes, her living on many levels of thought and emotion. It is authentic—time, place, inner life all blended. Yes, I admire her very much.[6]

This most interesting letter is doubly enlightening. On the one hand, it alerts us to the very real differences between Virginia Woolf and Ethel Wilson, and on the other it suggests the equally real similarities between Ethel Wilson and Arnold Bennett.

Virginia Woolf and Ethel Wilson have in common an essentially feminine sensibility, a responsiveness to the minutiae of daily life and to the finest nuances of human relationships. They also share a capacity to find symbolic suggestiveness in such things as the flight of birds, the ripple and flow of wind and water, the alternation of darkness and light. But they differ first of all in that Mrs. Wilson is far less interested in technical experimentation, in such modern devices as stream of consciousness and flashbacks, and secondly, and more importantly, in that Mrs. Wilson has a broader range of social sympathy. The charge has occasionally been made that Mrs. Wilson is imprisoned within the values of the affluent professional classes of Vancouver, but to anyone truly conversant with her work this charge is ridiculous. Whereas Mrs. Woolf was only really successful in creating characters from her own social class, Mrs. Wilson's greatest successes have been with such working class "heroines" as Myrtle and Vicky in *Tuesday and Wednesday,* Lilly in *Lilly's Story,* and Maggie Vardoe in *Swamp Angel.* There is scarcely a trace of snobbery or patronage in the whole body of her work, nothing that even approaches a patrician sneer.

This sympathetic concern with the poor and struggling, this ability to find elements of heroism in the apparently most unheroic of characters, is what links Ethel Wilson to Arnold Bennett. His *Old Wives' Tale* and *Riceyman Steps* have much in common with *Tuesday and Wednesday, Lilly's Story* and *Swamp Angel.* They share not only an interest in the struggling lower and lower middle classes, but also a concern with the unspectacular passage of time, a recognition of the importance of such daily routines as cooking and eating, an awareness of the significance of apparently insignificant events, an eye for the poetry behind the prose of everyday experience.

III *Family Background*

Ethel Wilson began to write relatively late in her life, and it is interesting to speculate why she, as a happily married and financially secure woman of middle age, happened to write at all. Married to an eminently successful Vancouver physician, Dr. Wallace Wilson, she was certainly not motivated by a need to make money.

Her family background had something to do with it. Born in South Africa of English parents, she was left an orphan when still a very small child, and was brought up by her maternal grandmother and by various aunts and uncles, first in Staffordshire in England, and, from the age of ten onwards, in Vancouver, British Columbia. Speaking of her father's family, she says, "Just as red hair occurs from time to time in families, or big thumbs, there was a tendency in my father's family towards writing—never very much, nor very good, but certainly never very bad, because they were a critical lot."[7] In another letter she records that when her father was a schoolboy in the village of Stickney in Lincolnshire, "his schoolmaster was a Frenchman called Paul Verlaine."[8] A half-sister of her father "became a journalist and Garvin's right-hand man on the *Observer*"[9]; another aunt translated Schumann, Pushkin and Spengler into English.[10] There were also literary connections on her mother's side of the family. As the opening chapter of *The Innocent Traveller* reveals, Matthew Arnold was a regular visitor to the home of her maternal grandparents, and Arnold Bennett was another friend of the family. In conversation, Mrs. Wilson has told me of occasional meetings with Arnold Bennett when she was a girl in Staffordshire. Of the maternal grandmother and other relatives with whom she grew up in Vancouver, she has written, "This family were not writers, but were certainly readers."[11]

Writing, then, was highly regarded on both sides of Mrs. Wilson's family. A more immediate cause of her own impulse to write may have been her knowledge of and love for Vancouver and British Columbia. Here was a city which in half a century had emerged from a virtual wilderness to a thriving metropolis, and a province whose natural beauty was unsurpassed; and yet no one had sought to record them in serious prose fiction. A few prose romances of British Columbia had appeared—notably A. M. Stephen's *The Kingdom of the Sun* (1927) and *The Gleaming Archway* (1929)—and a few romantic poems by Bliss Carman, Marjorie Pickthall, and Pauline Johnson, but no attempts had been made to capture the distinguishing features of Vancouver society, or to relate British Columbian life to its rugged but beautiful landscape and waterways. A desire to fill this vacuum is implied in Mrs. Wilson's own accounts of the beginnings of her literary career in "A Cat Among the Falcons":

> During the years before the war, 1937–38, I began to write. I did not contemplate a future in this occupation—life as it was seemed already full—yet now, for the first time, I found it imperative to write. In my childhood we had stood, in Vancouver, on a sort of subsoil of a culture which, as the forests came down, had been vaguely prepared by our fore-bears in the haste of building and earning. They had arrived at the water's edge with their violins and pianos, some books, some pictures, ideas, undoubted aspirations, opinions—or nothing whatever. Many had memories, no money and a dubious future. Suddenly a small public library was housed. Here was this subsoil of theirs and this was where we stood when I was a child.
>
> When, all these years later, it seemed imperative to me that I should write, I knew of no outlet for "my kind of thing" nor for an individual in Vancouver who was so looney as to think of writing, then. I sent some pieces to the *New Statesman* in London and they were published. Then the war closed down on us all.[12]

If we are right in concluding that one of Mrs. Wilson's motives was to record her delight in the British Columbian scene, it means that in some sense, she is a regional writer. She has expressed her admiration for the best kind of regional writing—that which is at once regional and universal—in this portion of a letter:

> Here we come up against region, or regionalism. Now I regard region as a very rich and potent affair in writing— for those writers who are affected by Place; some are not— as I'm sure you do—quite different from what we regard

as provincialism. I can only illustrate my clumsy remarks by great examples of regional writers. One may, of course, say that Proust really wrote about Time. But Proust took his text from Place—a room, a limited area of his particular Paris, the two little towns of Combray and Balbec. Yet he did not write *for* the reading public of these places or even *for* the French. He simply wrote (not "he wrote simply"— what a difference the placing of a word makes!), and the result is a book both regional and universal. Mark Twain did not write *for* the people of the Mississippi River, but his greatest book is regional and universal. He wrote of that region and of human nature in that region and he became part of larger literature because he wrote his story so truly and so well. Thomas Hardy, Emily Brontë—bounded narrowly by space, and unbounded in herself—there it is, writers of books that are both regional and universal, all writing with great and various power, but none of them writing with an eye on home or a national public. And so I think it should be in Canada. A "writer" simply writes. Our writing cannot but be Canadian, don't let us ever worry about that. But it can be good, or bad. That is what matters.[13]

That letter takes us from regionalism in literature to nationalism. I do not think that there was anything in the literary atmosphere of Canada in the mid-nineteen-thirties to impel Mrs. Wilson to write. The very fact that she submitted her first stories to the *New Statesman* is symptomatic: with the partial exception of the then struggling *Canadian Forum,* there was no literary magazine in Canada to which she could send them. During and immediately after World War II, however, there was something of a literary renaissance in Canada, and the hospitality which the late John Sutherland, as editor of *Northern Review,* gave to some of Ethel Wilson's early stories was undoubtedly a factor in encouraging her to persevere with her writing.[14] Ethel Wilson has been actively concerned with Canadian literature, as such of her essays as "A Cat Among the Falcons," "The Bridge or the Stokehold?" "A Series of Combination of Events . . . ," and "Of Alan Crawley" demonstrate, but she has been more concerned with its quality than with its national character. Again I quote one of her letters:

Now about Canadian literature. Here I know what I think.
I have to be bold to take myself as the nearest available
example of a Canadian who writes, although my output is
so small as not to prove anything. Although I know other
countries, I am Canadian and so I could not write anything
that convinced myself (of any length) that is not Canadian
in aspect. I do not choose this; it is inevitable. I know Canada
from here [Vancouver] to Prince Edward Island, but I
could not write anything (of any length) except about
British Columbia—places and persons. I don't choose it; it's
inevitable. (Of course I suppose one's heart is involved. It's
my region.) And yet, although the writing of a Canadian
is almost bound to be Canadian in character, and perhaps
(I only say perhaps) should be, I feel strongly that no one,
Canadian or other, should write *for* Canadians—or *for* Aus-
tralians, or *for* Americans. A writer, I should think, simply
writes from the faith (not to speak too solemnly) that is
in him. If one writes as a Canadian writing *for* Canadians,
I think one runs grave risk of becoming provincial, and of
thereby limiting Canadian literature. The writer is an individual first, but of a national complexion, whether he likes
it or not.[15]

Mrs. Wilson also touched on this question of literary nationalism
in two of her essays, "The Cat Among the Falcons" and "The
Bridge or the Stokehold?" In the former she expressed her hope
for Canadian literature—"My hope is that with the help of initially
sound and natural individual processes we may in Canadian letters attain that honour which shall make us at least heirs of
time"[16]—and her fear that courses in Creative Writing might ruin
it:

And so, the course known as "Creative Writing" renders me
uneasy and year by year I am apprehensive lest the results
in our country may be marked by a current mode or—
contrariwise—a straining after difference, and lest our writing may become derivative and undistinguished. These
courses can stimulate and give pleasure, and that is great
gain; but the odds are there. It is a brand of study not
indigenous here, I believe, but it is sporadic on this continent and will increase, whether I like it or not. I first

recognized, unforgettably and years ago, the echoes of a Thomas Wolfe manqué in productions from our neighbour's house, and I have since heard other echoing sounds.[17]

In "The Bridge or the Stokehold?" she reiterates the view expressed in the above letter that the writer must be a writer first and a Canadian writer second:

> It seems to me that the problems of the stoker (or the craftsman, or the artist) are universal, for people who are writers are first writers, and then they are Canadian writers, Polish, French, Russian, English writers. I understand so well what the Canadian novelist Mordecai Richler said when he was asked, "Are you a Jewish writer or a Canadian writer?"
>
> He answered, "Neither. I am a writer," Yet he is a Canadian writer, and so am I.[18]

IV *Her Reception*

These, then, were some of the convictions with which Ethel Wilson embarked on a writing career in 1937. She was convinced that the merely fashionable or the merely strange in writing is wrong, that economy is one of the hallmarks of good writing, that one must seek to write matter-of-factly and without pretentiousness, and that the best writing combines involvement and detachment, deep feeling and scepticism. Supported in her enterprise by a family which valued literature, she had as her *donnée* a background of wide reading and an intimate knowledge of the people, landscape, flora and fauna of her adopted British Columbia.

Her writing was an immediate, though never an overwhelmingly popular, success. Her early stories were readily accepted by such English periodicals as the *New Statesman* and *Orion*; she paused in her writing during the War; in the immediate post-War years she wrote the first of her novels, *Hetty Dorval*, (1947) and began to contribute stories to John Sutherland's *Northern Review*, then the leading literary magazine of Canada. Although most reviewers had reservations about *Hetty Dorval*, mentioning its slightness and its touches of melodrama, they all recognized it as a first novel of great promise. For *The Innocent Traveller*,

(1949) praise was almost unanimous; typical was C. M. Brown's comment in the *Saturday Review of Literature* that the book "is gentle, engaging, quietly wise, and nostalgic without being dated."[19] Reviews of *The Equations of Love* (1952) supported the claim of the *Canadian Forum* that with this book she had "really arrived."[20] The *New York Times* reviewer, Stuart Keate, said that "Mrs. Wilson tells *Lilly's Story*, the American title of the book, with infinite tenderness, wit and perception, and with economy of words." He continued:

> In a few magic strokes, she is able to illuminate a mood or a life: a movement in a darkened hall; a child's-eye view of a fight among eagle, robin and snake; a first revelation of love to an unnoticed mother, as she watches her daughter greet her husband. The result is a moving and eloquent saga.[21]

The critical reaction to *Swamp Angel* (1954) was almost equally enthusiastic. L. A. G. Strong, writing in *The Spectator*, best defined the nature of the book when he said:

> The telling is smooth, the tone of voice is low, the language economical; yet from the quiet but powerful opening to the last Excalibur flight of Swamp Angel the story troubles the mind with overtones and reticences, as if each chapter were a moon with a hidden side more important than the one which Mrs. Wilson shows us.[22]

In view of the very favourable reception of these earlier books, it is strange that *Love and Salt Water* (1956) and *Mrs. Golightly and Other Stories* (1961) were reviewed almost exclusively in Canada. Even in her own country, *Love and Salt Water* received only tepid approval, but the short stories were highly praised. The most perceptive review of *Mrs. Golightly* was probably that of Patricia Gallagher in the *Tamarack Review*, who wrote in part:

> Mrs. Wilson has insight and objectivity and a remarkable talent for distilling the essence of a situation so that glimpsing the world through her eyes we see more subtlety of character, more love, fear, confusion, tenderness and bitterness— more of human feeling and human relationship than we could ever see with our own eyes. She is a verbal painter

whose pictures are often worth a thousand words from lesser craftsmen.[23]

In spite of such favourable reviews, Mrs. Wilson's books have never sold in large quantities: her sales have been measured in the thousands rather than the tens of thousands. They have, however, earned the praise of the discriminating, and *The Equations of Love* was published not only in Canada, the United States, and England but also, in translation, in Switzerland, Italy, and Denmark.

Her quiet dedication to literature and her high standards of craftsmanship have brought Mrs. Wilson several honours. An honorary degree of Doctor of Letters was conferred on her by the University of British Columbia in 1955; she was awarded a special medal by The Canada Council in 1961; and she was given the Lorne Pierce Gold Medal by the Royal Society of Canada in 1964. In presenting her for the latter award, Professor Carl F. Klinck said in part:

> Mrs. Wilson is a "born watcher," a novelist with unusual ability to observe, to understand, and to record for "the outward eye and the inward eye." Readers have found her special qualities to be enchantment, sensitivity, humour, warmth, and "forthright feminine feeling." The introduction to a little girl, Topaz, a character in *The Innocent Traveller*, is a favourite example. Topaz, "who could not be squelched," is "perched there on top of two cushions, as innocent as a poached egg."
>
> Some readers, impressed chiefly by the delightful surface of her stories, have thought of Mrs. Wilson herself as "the innocent traveller." But those who recognize also her strong sense of place, time, and circumstance agree with Professor Watters when he pays tribute to her as "the experienced traveller." Avoiding the shallows of sentimentality, Mrs. Wilson offers not only vivacity, wit, and the play of social manners, but also an intelligent awareness of the deep entanglements in human relationships. She has the wisdom, the personality, and the art of a mature story-teller.[24]

I hope to demonstrate the truth of this perceptive tribute in the following pages.

CHAPTER 2

Short Stories and Essays

I Short Stories

ETHEL Wilson's literary career began with the writing and publication of short stories and it therefore seems proper to begin our study with them, even though her only book of stories, *Mrs. Golightly and Other Stories*[1] (1961), was the last of her books to appear. In the short stories, moreover, may be seen ideas, attitudes and techniques which will recur in her novels.

Mrs. Wilson has published to date eighteen short stories, sixteen of which are contained in *Mrs. Golightly* (which also includes two essays). Two stories, "A Simple Translation" and "A Visit to the Frontier," have appeared since *Mrs. Golightly* was published. In addition, some sections of Mrs. Wilson's novels were originally published in periodicals as short stories: "The Innumerable Laughter," for example, from *The Innocent Traveller*, and "Miss Tritt," from "Tuesday and Wednesday" in *The Equations of Love*.

The stories may be roughly subdivided into three categories: those dominated by a sense of humour, those dominated by a sense of horror, and a third group in which humour and horror exist side by side. The primarily humorous group includes "Mrs. Golightly and the First Convention," "God help the young fishman," and "I Just Love Dogs"; the stories in which horror is almost unrelieved are "Haply the soul of my grandmother," "From Flores," "The Birds," "The Fog," "Hurry, hurry," "Mr. Sleepwalker," "Beware the Jabberwock, my son . . . beware the Jubjub bird," "Till death us do part," "The Window," and "A Visit to the Frontier"; stories in which humour and horror are more or less evenly balanced are "We have to sit opposite," "A drink with

Adolphus," and "Truth and Mrs. Forrester." Two relatively brief and slight stories, "On Nimpish Lake" and "A Simple Translation" do not fit any of these categories: the former is a glimpse of two brothers living in a remote but beautiful part of the interior of British Columbia, and the latter a fantasy about an elderly lady who dies and finds her life in heaven singularly like her life on earth. But the categories are far from rigid: even the most purely humorous stories have undertones of horror, and the horrible ones are lightened with irony and tenderness. Together the stories aptly illustrate the epigraph of *Mrs. Golightly*, taken from Edwin Muir's *The Difficult Land:* "Life '. . . is a difficult country, and our home.' "

A. *The Theme of Isolation*

The most common protagonist in these stories—she appears in at least half of them—is a married woman of the upper middle class in or from Vancouver. She is usually a woman of middle age, married to a professional man who is frequently absent on various business enterprises, and she is therefore rather lonely and insecure. Her name varies—Mrs. Golightly, Mrs. Forrester, Mrs. Gormley, Miriam, Mrs. Manly, Lucy—but she is obviously Mrs. Wilson herself, or her *alter ego*. This is not a fault, for it simply indicates that Mrs. Wilson is observing the sound rule of writing out of her own experience. There is nothing offensively egotistical in these stories: Mrs. Wilson has the happy knack of regarding herself with ironic detachment. Moreover, the range of her sympathy is indicated by the variety of protagonists in the other short stories: an eleven-year-old country boy, a middle-aged sea-captain, a young fish merchant, an old impoverished woman, a male bookseller, a young female shop clerk, a wealthy retired businessman, a little old lady. Unlike Virginia Woolf, whose imaginative sympathy was almost entirely restricted to members of her own social class, Ethel Wilson has the capacity to enter imaginatively into the lives of people of very different backgrounds and attitudes.

The common denominator of Mrs. Wilson's protagonists is their loneliness, or their sense of alienation from their fellows. The sense of individual isolation is the chief difficulty of "the difficult land," and mutual love, especially the love of a happy marriage,

the chief means of overcoming it. The humour of "Mrs. Golightly and the First Convention" turns upon her sense of being
out of place among the other, more sophisticated, convention
wives, and although the treatment here is light and almost
farcical there is no doubt that a basic seriousness underlies the
witty surface. In "Haply the soul of my grandmother," Mrs.
Forrester is driven to the verge of hysterical panic by her sense
of the alien nature of Egyptian religion and society, while in
"On Nimpish Lake" the two brothers come to feel a sense of
alienation from the environment to which they have grown accustomed because of their glimpse of the freedom of the visiting
Mr. Leander. "From Flores," the story of a fatal shipwreck,
presents us with a quadruple separation: Captain Findlay Crabbe
yearns to be reunited with his wife, the crewman Ed wants to
be with his cronies at Port Alberni, the young passenger Jason
longs to join his pregnant girlfriend, and the little Indian boy
who is being taken to the hospital is anxiously sought by his parents; but all these reunions are prevented when the ship sinks
in a sudden storm.

A superficially light treatment of this theme of human isolation is found again in "God help the young fishman." The
complacent middle-class housewives who badger the young fish
merchant with extravagant and contradictory orders have no
understanding of his common humanity: to them he is a mere
instrument, rather than an individual. A more complex and
powerful treatment occurs in "We have to sit opposite." Here
two Vancouver matrons find themselves sitting opposite a German family in a train; at first they are merely amused and slightly
disconcerted by the Germans' vulgarity and discourtesy, and
attempt to retaliate by telling the Germans tall tales about
Canada; but as the story proceeds there is a mounting sense of
horror. The Germans become the embodiments of all the prejudice and cruelty of Nazi totalitarianism, and we realize that the
space between the train seats symbolizes an unbridgeable gulf
between two ways of life.

The isolation is on a smaller, more individual, scale in "The
Birds," "Fog," "Hurry, hurry," "Truth and Mrs. Forrester," "Mr.
Sleepwalker," "Beware the Jabberwock," "Till death do us part,"
"The Window," and "A Visit to the Frontier." In "The Birds"
the breakdown of a love affair is compared to the death of a

bird when it shatters its body against the glass of a window: the effort of one human being to establish connection with another has been destroyed by an invisible but powerful barrier. "A drink with Adolphus" describes a cocktail party at which people, seemingly so "together," prove to inhabit separate worlds between which there is virtually no communication. In "Fog," an old woman lives and dies in isolation: people, it is implied, are like ships in a fog, warning others by their foghorns to keep off.

There is a double loneliness in "Hurry, hurry." Miriam, the story's protagonist, is another in the series of wives whose husbands are absent, and her fear of the strange man she encounters on a remote area of the British Columbia coast is enhanced by her isolation. The man proves to be a murderer, and at the end of the story we become aware of *his* pathetic loneliness as he runs "across the tussocky field, stumbling, half blind, sobbing, crying out loud." "Truth and Mrs. Forrester," on the other hand, is another demonstration of the isolation which can be felt as easily in society as in the wilderness. Mrs. Forrester goes through a busy day of social relationships, but there is no real communication between her and her guests: she is merely playing the part of a hostess, while inwardly she worries over the safety of her absent husband.

The frequent absence of her husband, who is on war service, is also a powerful factor in Mrs. Manly's sense of alienation in the haunting story, "Mr. Sleepwalker." Wherever she goes, Mrs. Manly keeps encountering this strange little man who smells like a fox or rotten wood, and when he finally turns up at her apartment as a salesman she attacks him with a vase. The man proves to be a harmless, pathetic creature; again human beings have demonstrated their incapacity to overcome their essential solitude.

That words, the only bridges between people, can often be a barrier rather than a bridge, is demonstrated in "Beware the Jabberwock . . . ," where it is his wife's continual chattering that drives Tom Krispin temporarily to desert his wife. And even the family, ordinarily conceived as the chief bulwark against loneliness, can be a destructive force on occasion: seeing how horribly Kate, her fellow-clerk, is tied to her drunken mother, the narrator of "Till death do us part" turns to a mediocre marriage in search of a modicum of comfort.

There is no such thing as self-sufficiency. Mr. Willy, in "The

Window," is wealthy, leisured, has a house with a beautiful view, but he comes to realize that isolation from one's fellows is a fate worse than death: "He must in some way and very soon break the great wall that shuts him off from whatever light there might be. Not for fear of death oh God not for fear of death but for fear of something else." (p. 209)

But death is the great divider, and it is fitting that the latest of Mrs. Wilson's stories, "A Visit to the Frontier," should deal with the isolating power of death. In this story (based, Mrs. Wilson tells me in a letter, on an actual nightmare she experienced)[2] a happily married couple are riding in a train in Western Canada when there is a sudden wreck. The rest of the story records the dream-like sensations of the dying wife as she vainly seeks her husband, and the poignancy is almost unbearable.

B. *The Sense of Place*

If the theme of isolation is the chief unifying factor among the short stories of Ethel Wilson, a secondary one is their strong sense of place. One of the ways in which individuals mitigate their sense of loneliness is by firmly attaching themselves to a familiar and beloved environment. Mrs. Wilson herself obviously has such an attachment to Vancouver in particular, and to British Columbia and to Canada in general. At least half of her stories are at least partially set in Vancouver itself, three are set in other parts of British Columbia, "A Visit to the Frontier" is set in the prairies and foothills of Western Canada, and the three stories set in other parts of the world have Vancouverites as their main characters. In several of the stories, notably "On Nimpish Lake," "A drink with Adolphus," "Fog," "Hurry, hurry," and "The Window," suggestive descriptions of the scenery and climate of British Columbia play a large part in creating the atmosphere. The descriptions are always exact, and reveal a trained eye not only for the contour and colour of the landscape but also for the flora and fauna of the region. They are never merely set-pieces of description, however, but always, by creating mood and suggesting theme, form an organic part of the story. Here, for example, is a passage from "On Nimpish Lake":

Nimpish Lake is far to find. You drive inland for a day, and then next morning you leave the rugged highway and drive on a narrow winding road through the sage brush along waggon tracks, over the cattle ranges, up into the hills through the forest of crowded little pines. The forest seems quiet. You think there is little life in these high woods, for you see and hear no birds there. But perhaps you hear a chipmunk scolding or you see a squirrel carrying great whiskers of grass dried by the summer. He is making his winter home. He needs plenty of grass, because in these parts winter is long and severe for little hibernating creatures. When you reach the cabin beside Nimpish Lake you will see the gray whiskey-jacks who love the neighborhood of man—what cheeky birds they are and how endearing—and magpies sometimes, and the pretty kingfisher, the osprey and the eagle. The rapacious hawk keeps to the open country. Before you see the lake through the trees you will hear the loons laughing and crying on the water. The loon is the true owner of the lake, and the loon's melodious unhappy cry is the true voice of these regions.

(pp. 29–30)

Not only does this passage reveal Mrs. Wilson's knowledge of the region, and enable us to put her characters in a physical setting, it also prefigures the sadness of the two brothers who, at the end of the story, long for the the freedom of the wild geese to escape, at least for a season, the isolation of this remote lake country.

The recognition of their isolation is in fact all that "happens" in "On Nimpish Lake," and in this respect the story is typical of Mrs. Wilson's plots. The plots are simple and straightforward for the most part, seldom involving much complexity of event or sudden twists of surprise, but eventuating rather in a moment of recognition or awareness, an epiphany, to borrow Joyce's word, or a moment of vision, to borrow Conrad's phrase. Even when violent events do occur, such as the murders in "Hurry, hurry" and "Fog," or the train wreck in "A Visit to the Frontier," the events are either played down or take place off-stage. Mrs. Wilson is not interested so much in events as in their psychological implications, their emotional reverberations.

C. *Theory and Technique*

The only explicit discussion of the art of the short story by
Ethel Wilson occurs in an "Address to the Students of the School
of Architecture, U.B.C." In that address she said:

> There is the short story which is a curiously interesting
> art form enormously dependent within its small compass on
> structure. If structure is faulty a short story may be all at
> sea, as a well-intentioned ship whose rudder is faulty is all
> at sea. The ship and the story will probably not arrive at
> their desired destinations. Paradoxically, too slavish and
> careful a structure may destroy a short story. The earnest
> student of the short story who tries too hard to conform to
> some required shape or tension or termination, or experienced
> practitioners who have come to use a certain formula or
> mould, are endangered by the mould or formula becoming
> apparent, and then the story has no life. It does not "hap-
> pen," and I think a short story has to "happen." Some years
> ago a student of the art or craft of the short story attended
> classes held by a young visiting lecturer and delighted me.
> The young lecturer was himself going through the "symbol"
> stage, and injected the awful power of symbol even into
> the trivia of the short story. Symbol became only a fashion
> and the stories became overloaded. The student was be-
> wildered. He said to a friend of mine, "With all this symbol,
> I've got so that I can't look at a boiled egg without blush-
> ing!" This impedes work, as well it might. The short story is
> slippery—hard to catch and hold in the hand. I have written
> a few short stories, and observe with respect and some
> pleasure the opportunity for economy of expression, for
> the recognition of line and contour, and the open oppor-
> tunity for inference. The short story is a strong, delicate and
> tricky art, almost done with mirrors. I admit that, but cannot
> take a lively interest in it. You will agree that nothing is more
> unsatisfactory to the writer or the reader than a blown-up,
> or too sentimental, or self-conscious, or pretentious, or in-
> dustriously symbolic short story. I think that any fashion in
> short story writing is poor fashion and I cannot see that any

specific structure can safely be prescribed if the art is to remain free. The artlessness of de Maupassant—of O. Henry's *The Municipal Report*, Somerset Maugham's *Rain*, of Anatole France's *The Procurator of Judea*—that artlessness is very artful indeed.[3]

The four chief points which arise from that discussion are her concern for structure, her emphasis on a vivid sense of reality, her suspicion of an overuse of symbolism and her preference for an artful artlessness. It would be useful to relate these matters to her own practice of the short story form.

While recognizing the importance of structure, Mrs. Wilson is concerned that it should not become rigid or mechanical. Her own stories exhibit great skill and variety in this regard. Take, for example, that very important structural element, the beginning. Some of her stories begin with character introductions, some with dialogue, some with descriptions of setting, and some with action. The beginnings are always brisk, direct and unpretentious, and at the same time suggestive and relevant. The opening paragraph of "Mrs. Golightly and the First Convention," for example, sets the lady and her husband before us in a beautifully economical series of short, simple, ironic sentences:

> Mrs. Golightly was a shy woman. She lived in Vancouver. Her husband, Tommy Golightly, was not shy. He was personable and easy to like. He was a consulting engineer who was consulted a great deal by engineering firms, construction firms, logging firms in particular, any firm that seemed to have problems connected with traction. When he was not being consulted he played golf, tennis, or bridge according to whether the season was spring, summer, autumn or winter. Any time that was left over he spent with his wife and three small children of whom he was very fond. When he was with them, it seemed that that was what he liked best. He was a very extroverted sort of man, easy and likeable, and his little wife was so shy that it just was not fair.
>
> (p. 1)

In "Haply the soul of my grandmother," on the other hand, Mrs. Forrester's opening remark—"It is airless"—establishes at once the claustrophobic atmosphere that is to dominate that story. We

have already observed how the descriptive passage with which
"On Nimpish Lake" opens indicates the basic theme of the story.
"From Flores," the fourth story in the book, opens with action—
the always interesting action of setting out on a journey. The
details—the red shirt, the rocky point, the isolated family—are
selected to establish the ominous mood of the story and the theme
of human vulnerability and isolation:

> Up at Flores Island, Captain Findlay Crabbe readied his
> fishboat the *Effie Cee* for the journey home and set out in
> good spirits while the weather was fair. But even by the
> time he saw the red shirt flapping like mad from the rocky
> point just north of the Indian's place the wind had freshened.
> Nevertheless Fin Crabbe told the big man at the wheel to
> turn into shore because there must be some trouble there
> and that Indian family was pretty isolated. As the man at
> the wheel turned the nose of the boat towards the shore, the
> skipper listened to the radio. The weather report was good,
> and so he went out on the small deck well satisfied and stood
> there with his hands on his hips, looking at the shore where
> the red flag was.
>
> (p. 34)

From these straightforward but suggestive beginnings, the
stories always build swiftly and surely to a meaningful climax.
Look, for example, at "Hurry, hurry." The opening paragraph of
description creates a sense of nature's magnitude, majesty and
vague menace, suggests something strange, elusive and misleading, evokes the passing of time and the transitoriness of beauty
and innocence. The second paragraph brings out Miriam's loneliness, while the third paragraph, with its reference to soldier blackbirds, stubble fields, salt wind, whimpering sandpipers, teasing
terriers, and marshy blackish sand, suggests cruelty, pursuit, wild-
ness, and fear. Gradually the atmosphere of tension builds up as
we watch the great solitary crane settle among the stakes and
rushes, hear the strange grating cry of the blackbirds, see the
large wounded hawk lying at the edge of the salt-water ditch.
Prepared by all this, we literally wince as does Miriam when the
strange man appears and babbles his deceitful story of there being
a cougar up ahead.
    The ending is the only part of "Hurry, hurry" about which I am

not altogether happy. We are violently switched from Miriam's point of view to that of an omniscient narrator as we read:

> Far behind them along the dyke the body of the young woman who had just been murdered lay humped beside the salt-water ditch.
>
> The man who had killed her reached the cover of the hedge, out of sight of that woman with the dogs. When he reached the cover of the hedge he began to run across the tussocky field, stumbling, half blind, sobbing, crying out loud.
>
> (p. 110)

It is difficult to suggest an alternative to this switch in point of view if we are to be apprised of the event, but it does savour of the sort of "tricky art, almost done with mirrors" in which Mrs. Wilson professes to have no interest.

Although such trick endings are rare in Mrs. Wilson's stories, her endings are not quite as successful as her beginnings. There is something slightly forced about the ending of "On Nimpish Lake," and something overly clever about the ending of "We have to sit opposite." The ending of "Fog" has a touch of that cloying sentimentality which often mars the endings of Katherine Mansfield's stories, and the final reference in "Mr. Sleepwalker" to Mrs. Manly as a hare makes the otherwise frightening references to the man as a fox seem slightly ridiculous in retrospect: the effect is to make something which we had been taking seriously suddenly become merely a clever game. The other stories, however, all end with unambiguous power, and almost always the manner in which the ending takes us back in imagination to the beginning gives to the stories a sense of completion, of achieved unity. In "From Flores," for example, the final picture of the Indian father walking forlornly up and down the Alberni docks brings the theme of the story into vivid focus, and at the same time reminds us of the way the story began with the red flag signalling the *Effie Cee* to the Indian encampment.

An important element in structure is point of view. To give a sense of unity to a short story, the single point of view is almost always preferable, and Mrs. Wilson uses it in no less than twelve of her eighteen short stories. She reveals her determination not to follow any one formula, however, by employing the alternating point of view in "A drink with Adolphus" and "Beware the Jabber-

wock . . .," and a multiple point of view in "On Nimpish Lake,"
"From Flores," and "We have to sit opposite." These exceptional
devices are always justified by the material she is presenting. The
alternating point of view, for example, is necessary in "A drink
with Adolphus" to establish the fact of human isolation: Mrs.
Gormley and Mrs. Leaper have been guests at the same party
and have witnessed essentially the same events, yet their interpre-
tations of them are almost entirely different. And in "We have to
sit opposite" the multiple point of view is similarly essential: if
the observation of Nazi vulgarity had been from the point of
view of one of the ladies only, we should have been less ready
to believe it, and we should have been deprived of the by-play
between the two Canadian ladies which makes the situation supportable for them.

Mrs. Wilson is similarly successful in giving to her stories that
sense of vivid immediacy which she describes in terms of "happening." In "Hurry, hurry," for example, we feel that we are
with Miriam every step of the way, and are as tense as she is
over what is to happen next. This effect is achieved largely by the
sensuous particularity of the writing: we see the mountains, feel
the west wind from the sea, hear the cry of the soldier blackbirds, smell the salt marsh. Mrs. Wilson always manages to
achieve this sense of a dramatic present, to convince us that
what is happening is really happening now, and that no one
can be sure what will happen next.

D. *Symbolism*

It is this quality of faithfully recording the actual stuff of experience which most impresses us about Mrs. Wilson's stories;
but there is also in them, despite her protestations, a certain
amount of symbolism. In "On Nimpish Lake," the wild geese at
the end are obviously symbolic of freedom, of a freedom which
the two isolated brothers envy. In "The Birds," the symbolism
of the window against which the birds shatter themselves is made
quite explicit:

> I looked out of the window at the living birds who were
> tossing themselves in the air and flying from tree to tree,
> and a moment of revelation came to me and I was a bird
> and the birds were I. The birds flew and flew with speed

and attack in the clear air, and in the clear window was reflected to them the familiar sky and the flowers and the trees, and so each day some little bird flew into this familiar reflection and dashed itself against the real glass and fell, with its mouth split and its bones broken by the passion of its flight. Here was the dim mark of its death. And yesterday I had bashed my head against the reality that was waiting for me, invisible, and had nearly broken my neck. The thought of the merry birds and the birds in the years to be, falling outside the window, sickened me. A bird is so free.

(p. 64)

As we have already noticed, the mountains which are described at the beginning of "Hurry, hurry" are symbolic of the transitory, shifting, deceptive quality of reality. In "Mr. Sleepwalker" the fox to which the strange little man is compared is symbolic of all the deceit, bestiality, and slyness of which humanity is capable. In "The Window," the great window with its splendid view is symbolic of Mr. Willy's deliberate isolation from humanity. These are the most obvious symbols, but throughout the stories there are many examples of incidental symbolism. The symbolism, however, is never obtrusive, pretentious, or laboured: Mrs. Wilson observes the world about her, and if her observations reveal objects which are capable of symbolic interpretation, so much the better. We never feel that she is engaged in deliberate symbol-hunting: the symbols arise naturally out of her faithful observation of reality.

In this respect as in all others, Mrs. Wilson reveals her artful artlessness. Except occasionally in the endings, there is nothing forced or overwrought about her stories. They begin casually, as if we were overhearing a conversation, and they proceed gently, delicately, and unobtrusively. The style is limpid, unemphatic, but invariably in good taste and in the most fitting tone. It is only if we deliberately stop to consider the style that we realize how carefully the words have been chosen, how cunningly they have been arranged to achieve the right rhythm and the proper tone. "A multitude of little sandpipers ran along the wet sands as if they were on wheels." ("Hurry, hurry," p. 107). The observation is precise, the image well chosen, the rhythm of the sentence suggests the rhythm of the running birds.

In her short stories, then, Mrs. Wilson's chief themes are loneliness and love, human vulnerability and tenacity, the juxtaposition in the world of innocence and cruelty, beauty and fear, and she treats these themes in a style that is straightforward but also suggestive, realistic but also poetic and symbolic. She sees human beings as lonely creatures who forever seek, and occasionally find, the comfort and sustaining power of mutual love, and nature as a setting which is at once beautiful and menacing. There is in her work a rich sense of the multiplicity of reality, and yet of a fundamental unity achieved by the cosmic rhythms of birth and death, flight and pursuit, growth and decay. Simple on the surface, and always gentle and casual in tone, her stories suggest far more than they explicitly state.

II *Essays*

Ethel Wilson has published only nine essays, which is a pity since she strikes one as a natural essayist. Her casual but beautifully controlled style, her keen sensory awareness, her shrewd insight into human character, her strong sense of place, her wit and ironic detachment—all of these are characteristics ideally suited to the essay form. Since she has travelled extensively, we might have expected her to write many travel sketches, and had she chosen to do so she might have been as successful as D. H. Lawrence, Aldous Huxley or Lawrence Durrell. In fact, she has written only one travel essay—"On a Portuguese Balcony."[4] The majority of her essays are literary essays, personal discussions of the art of writing or tributes to such literary associates as John Sutherland and Alan Crawley.

"On a Portuguese Balcony" indicates what a good travel essayist Mrs. Wilson might have become. She exhibits, for example, a discriminating sense of colour:

> The sea wall is of a cream and grey colour (I think) with blue shadows. Then comes the long lower white sea wall, dazzling in the sunshine which also lights brilliantly the faces of tall rose-coloured houses trimmed merrily with white; and there is the long line of palms. There must be a ramp, evidently, leading up to the road which is flanked by the tall houses—rose, white, and pale yellow, how the sun lights them!—and swirls round the point of land and up the coast, past the storm-washed lobster grounds, skirting the formid-

able open Atlantic ocean, up to the ancient fishing village of Nezaré—where the girls, bare-footed, wear crinoline skirts and the matrons are draped in longest Arabian black and the sailors wear plaid shirts, and the bright-coloured fishing boats are towed to sea by oxen—up to Oporto and beyond.[5]

She also reveals a gift for observing the idiosyncratic habits, gestures, dress, manner of work and play, and speech patterns of the Portuguese people. And at the same time that she observes the present scene with such accuracy, she comments knowingly but not pedantically upon Portuguese history. Perhaps above all, she shows herself capable of making us aware of herself as an observer and yet of never obtruding herself upon us or letting her own egotism obscure our view of the people and place. She is at once involved and detached, a guide who cares but does not lecture or preach. When she does not know, she admits her ignorance; when she does know, she offers us the information modestly.

The only other essay by Mrs. Wilson which approaches the form of a travel essay is "The corner of X and Y streets," which appears in *Mrs. Golightly and Other Stories*. It describes the events at a Soho street corner shortly after World War II, and is a brief epiphany in which we get a poignant sense of the mingled gaiety and sadness of human life by watching and listening to three amateur performers—an accordion player, a girl singer, and a male dancer. The piece is slight but memorable, a snapshot of a moment of time which is in a sense an epitome of all time.

The seven literary essays need not be considered at length here. Relevant passages from them have been cited in the introductory chapter, and indeed it is as a means of illuminating Mrs. Wilson's own practice as a writer that these essays are most valuable. In all of them she reveals her fastidious but light-hearted concern with craftsmanship, the breadth of her reading and the eclecticism of her tastes, her modesty about her own achievements and her sincere admiration of the achievements of others. In "A Cat Among the Falcons,"[6] for example, she refers to herself as an "under-educated person" and expresses her admiration of literary critics—not for Ethel Wilson the usual creative writer's contempt for the alleged parasitism of the critical process! Equally indicative of her humility is her tribute to Henry Condell and John

Heming,[7] editors of Shakespeare's First Folio, to whose graves in
the little churchyard of St. Mary the Virgin Aldermanbury she
made a reverent pilgrimage.

What strikes us most about these essays is Ethel Wilson's un-
affected delight in the variety of human nature. Whether writing
about her own ancestors, in "Reflections in a Pool,"[8] or about her
Canadian contemporaries, in "A Series of Combination of Events
and Where is John Goodwin"[9] and "Of Alan Crawley,"[10] she is
never unkind or malicious but always affirmative. She is ironic
at her own expense, but never at that of others. She admits that
she may be idealizing the late John Sutherland, courageous and
provocative editor of *Northern Review,* but it is clear that she
prefers to err on that side rather than on the side of cynicism. And
yet for all this there is nothing bland or unduly mild about these
essays—they are strong, witty, trenchant, but uniformly tolerant
and wise. The essays, in short, are the products of a sensitive
mind which is aware of its own values and preferences, but which
has no desire to magnify these values and preferences into universal laws. In reading her essays, we are aware of an implicit
dialogue, in which the writer's part is always good-natured and
yet shrewdly perceptive.

CHAPTER 3

Hetty Dorval (1947)

HETTY *Dorval*[1] is the kind of first novel we might have expected its unassuming author to write. It is short, only just over a hundred pages, the pages small and the print comfortably large; it is, on the surface at least, simple and straightforward in both plot and characterization; and its tone is one of gentle wonderment at the vagaries of human nature. Above all, it is a book that can either be read in a few hours as a pleasant diversion, or studied intently as a subtle consideration of some of the more profound questions of psychology and ethics.

I *Mystery without Melodrama*

Read merely as light entertainment, *Hetty Dorval* commends itself to us as a mystery story. It records the reactions of a young girl, Frankie Burnaby, to an older and reputedly wicked woman, Hetty Dorval. Frankie is only twelve years old when the novel opens, and Mrs. Dorval appears as a strange new inhabitant in the small British Columbia town of Lytton where Frankie goes to school. At first Frankie is dazzled by Hetty's beauty, but gradually she begins to have doubts about the woman's character.

Wherever Frankie goes—in Vancouver, where she is sent to a private school, on shipboard on the Atlantic Ocean, in London—she keeps encountering Hetty, and on each encounter she is both attracted and repelled. Always in the background are vague rumours of some horrible secret in the life of Mrs. Dorval, and it is only near the very close of the novel, when she appears to be on the point of marrying the young Englishman whom Frankie has come to love, that we learn of her illegitimate birth and of her involvement in a series of unsavoury affairs with rich and powerful men. Enigmatic to the end, Hetty, at the close of the novel, gives up all claim to Frankie's young man in order to marry a

wealthy German, Jules Stern. Whether she does this out of concern for Frankie's feelings or Rick's welfare, or out of pure selfishness, is left to our speculation.

Even if we look no deeper than this, there is much to admire
in *Hetty Dorval*. As a thriller of the less sensational variety it is
very well managed. Almost always we are shown rather than told:
we get a series of dramatic scenes, each clearly lit in the fore-
ground but with intriguing shadows in the background. The
opening scene shows us Frankie and her girlfriend Ernestine
watching the arrival of Mrs. Dorval's furniture at the railway-
station, and mistaking Hetty's housekeeper, Mrs. Broom, for Hetty
herself. The second main scene describes the first meeting of
Frankie and Hetty; the third the arrival of the supposed *Mr.*
Dorval; the fourth, the town fair; and so on, right up until the
final confrontation of Frankie and Hetty, when the latter decides
for Jules Stern rather than Rick. The point is that each of these
scenes is a unit in itself, a satisfying and self-contained encounter,
and yet each points forward to the next and backward to its
predecessor. There is a closely linked sequence of dramatic episodes, in each of which a moment of time is clearly and percep-
tively limned, and in each of which the level of narrative interest
or suspense perceptibly rises.

An example may make clear how effectively Mrs. Wilson manages this narrative level of her work. Here is part of the opening
scene:

> The day that Mrs. Dorval's furniture arrived in Lytton,
> Ernestine and I had gone to the station to see the train come
> in. It was a hot day. The heat of the sun burned down from
> above, it beat up from the ground and was reflected from the
> hot hills. Mr. Miles, the station agent, was in his shirt-sleeves;
> the station dog lay and panted, got up, moved away, lay
> down and panted again; and the usual Indians stood leaning
> against the corners of the wooden station (we called it "the
> deepo") in their usual curious incurious fashion, not looking
> as though they felt the heat or anything else. The Indians
> always looked as though they had nothing to do, and per-
> haps they had nothing to do. Ernestine and I had nothing
> much to do, but school was out and supper wasn't ready and
> so we had drifted over to the station. Neither of our mothers

liked us to do this every day; but we were not absolutely forbidden.

When the train clanked in, a number of the stifling passengers got out seeking coolness in the bright glaring heat of the station platform. Ernestine and I watched these passengers with experienced eyes and saw that there was no one interesting to us. We did not find grown-ups interesting, but were always on the look-out for other children or for dogs. And sure enough there at the end of the train was a large dog, perhaps a Newfoundland, hot in his hot coat. The train men had got him out of a freight car, and then they heaved and pushed and lifted out a huge crated object that might be a piano, and then they got out packing case after packing case.

Directly the great dog stood upon the platform, looking sadly and nobly about him, a woman moved up to him and said casually, "Well, Sailor," and you might almost say the dog smiled. His thick bell-rope of a tail swung and he moved up to the woman who patted him lightly but gave her full attention to the crates and packing cases that the train hands and station hands deposited upon the platform. Ernestine and I had seen this woman before in the Lytton main street, but she was really the kind of woman that you don't notice. You might see her in a village, or in a big city, or in a streetcar, or on a train, and you would never notice. Nevertheless, we now saw that she had authority. She was dressed in dark grey. Her hair was dark grey too, and was taken straight back from her plain strong face. Suddenly she began to be interesting to Ernestine and to me, because she belonged to Sailor the dog and to all the new packing cases. (pp.1-2)

The very first sentence of that passage suggests a strong element in Hetty Dorval's appeal for Frankie: Frankie is a girl living in a town so small and so isolated that the arrival of the daily train is an event, and to her simple mind Mrs. Dorval represents the exotic, the sophisticated, and the mysterious. (This opening, too, recalls the beginning of Willa Cather's short story, "The Sculptor's Funeral," although the stories develop very differently.) The whole of the opening paragraph suggests oppressive boredom—the heat, the panting dog pointlessly moving from place to place, the leaning Indians, the idly drifting girls—and makes us long for

something to happen. The last sentence of the first paragraph
prefigures what is to be one of the main tensions in the plot—
that between the innocent freedom of a child's response and the
suspicious restraint of a parent's.

In the second paragraph, the appearance of the Newfoundland
dog and of the piano crate and other packing cases heightens the
effect of something strange, mysterious and almost monstrous
intruding into this sleepy little way-station. And when, in the
third paragraph, we see the woman go up to the dog and call
him Sailor, we at once jump to the false conclusion, as do the
girls, that this woman is Mrs. Dorval and that, having a huge
dog with such a name, she is a woman of the world and a woman
of strong will.

There are other things in these opening paragraphs that might
be commented upon. They reveal, for example, Mrs. Wilson's
talent for selective and suggestive description of landscape, her
fascination with animals and with people's gestures, and the deceptive simplicity of her style. But what I wish mainly to remark
here is the sheer cleverness of them from the point of view of
arousing suspense. Almost every sentence makes a statement but
at the same time raises a question. Who is Mrs. Dorval? Will
she be on the train? Is this dog hers? Is that a piano? Her piano?
Is that woman Mrs. Dorval? Why had the girls not really noticed
her before?

To initiate and sustain suspense on this level, and yet never
to deviate into melodrama, is not easy. There are, it is true, in
this first novel one or two scenes that come near to melodrama,
the chief one being that in which the housekeeper, Mrs. Broom,
introduced in the paragraphs first quoted as the woman in dark
grey, reveals that she is in fact Hetty Dorval's mother. Here is
the main part of that scene:

> And here Hetty made the mistake of her life. She laughed
> and said lightly, "I never had a mother either, and I've got on
> very nicely without one!"
> It was at that moment that Mrs. Broom moved forward
> out of the shadows and stood and leaned with her strong
> rough hands on the table in that circle of the lamplight. The
> whole room seemed to turn towards her, and we turned to-
> wards her, and she took all the power and meaning out of

the room into herself. And she began to shake.

Hetty and I stared at this controlled woman who stood shaking by the table, steadying herself with her strong hands flat on the table within the circle of the lamplight. I stood up straight and saw her hands square and rough and the fingers short and square-tipped pressed down hard upon the table to prevent their shaking as Mrs. Broom was shaking. The lower part of Mrs. Broom's face was in shadow but on her forehead I saw the veins stand out on the temples and then I saw that the whole face was distorted. I cannot tell you how horrible this was and how frightening to see this woman of wood and of closed doors opened violently from within with great suddenness and without reason. Hetty put her hands on the couch each side of her and leaned backwards as though to spring away. She looked in horror at Mrs. Broom who, still leaning forward on the table, struggled to compose herself.

"Mouse, what is it?" breathed Hetty. "What is it?"

I did not put out a hand to help Mrs. Broom because I saw that though she was racked and shaken physically, the thing that had caused this convulsion was not physical—and I did not know what it was.

Mrs. Broom spoke to Hetty, hoarsely and with effort. "Say what you said before!"

"What I said before?" said Hetty, bewildered. "I don't know what I said before."

"Then I'll tell you," said Mrs. Broom, who was gaining control of herself. "You said, 'I never had a mother, and I got along very well without one.'"

"Well, I *did* get along very well without one—thanks to you of course, Mouse," added Hetty generously.

Mrs. Broom looked on Hetty and said, "Hester . . . I am your mother," and the silence in the room was as though drums had stopped beating.

Hetty went quite white and stared at Mrs. Broom as though she had never seen her before, and perhaps she never had. I saw her breast heave as though she had been running.

"Mouse," she said at last, "that's not true!"

"Hester, I am your mother," repeated Mrs. Broom som-

brely. "Many's the time I've near told you and now I've
done it."

"Why . . ." said Hetty, and then she stopped. "Who . . ."
And she stopped again. "Mouse, you can't prove it!"

"Prove it!" said Mrs. Broom scornfully, "I've no call to
prove it, and I don't have to prove it. You're my daughter,
Hester, and you've brought me nothing but trouble from the
minute you could speak and you've never given me any
real love." (pp. 101-2)

Now, if one is reading the novel merely for its lively plot, that
may be accepted as a melodramatic fragment coming appropri-
ately enough at the climax of the action. But if one is reading the
novel a little more seriously, one may see that this scene is a
cunningly constructed link in the whole narrative chain. It is, in
fact, one of those scenes from which we get the shock of recognition. For, from the very first, we have seen Mrs. Broom protect-
ing and directing Hetty with maternal solicitude, and only Mrs.
Wilson's narrative skill has diverted us from asking why a mere
housekeeper should so long and so stoutly defend such a woman
from the world. Mrs. Broom's dark grey has been a shade in the
background which has been waiting all along for Mrs. Wilson to
illuminate it. And what prevents the illumination from being
really melodramatic is the very steadiness of the beam when it
finally does shine out. There is no vague rush of uncontrolled
emotion, but a disciplined delineation of physical detail denoting
psychological strain. There is no wild waving of the arms, but
rather "fingers short and square-tipped pressed down hard upon
the table."

II *Place*

But there is more to *Hetty Dorval* than a plot which is intricately woven and cunningly controlled. First of all, there is evident here as in all of Mrs. Wilson's work a rich sense of place.
I do not mean only, although this is part of it, that Mrs. Wilson
is a good regionalist. Certainly she does give us a sense of what
it is like to live in the British Columbia which has been her home
since childhood. She is not one of those authors who are afraid
of naming their places, who seek to give a kind of vague uni-
versality to their settings. When she wants to describe the Thomp-

son River she calls it the Thompson River, and proceeds to describe it as she has seen it:

> Anybody looking out of the front windows of Mrs. Dorval's
> bungalow could look down on to the racing Thompson River.
> Perhaps the water was emerald, perhaps it was sapphire.
> It is both. It is neither. It is a brilliant river, blue-green
> with lacings of white foam and spray as the water hurls
> itself violently along in rapids against hidden or projecting
> rocks, a rapid, racing, calling river. The hills rise high and
> lost on each side of the banks. These hills are traversed
> hardly at all. There is no reason to climb, to scale the top,
> to look down. In the sunlight the dun-coloured gorges of
> the blue-green river look yellow and ocherous, and in some
> places there are outcroppings of rock that are nearly rose
> red. Large dark and solitary pine trees give landmark and
> meaning. . . . As evening comes on, the hills grow dove grey
> and purple; they take on a variety of surprising shapes and
> shades, and the oblique shafts of sunlight disclose new hills
> and valleys which in daylight merge into one and are not
> seen. (pp. 3–4)

That is good regionalist writing, for it catches the distinctive qualities of the region: the speed of its rivers, its high, lonely hills, its dark and solitary pine-trees. But it is more than that: the description is an organic part of the atmosphere of the whole novel. The tumultuous river is symbolic, to the young girl Frankie, of Hetty Dorval herself—something powerful, mysterious, almost monstrous, but at the same time very beautiful. And the mysteriousness of the hills at evening, their "variety of surprising shapes and shades," "the oblique shafts of sunlight" disclosing "new hills and valleys," suggests the multifaceted mystery of Mrs. Dorval, whose effect upon Frankie is slightly different if equally baffling every time that she sees her.

Mrs. Wilson's descriptive gifts do not only extend to the landscape of her home region. In this novel she makes us feel the reality not alone of British Columbia but also of the Atlantic Ocean, of the Cornish coast, of London, and of Paris. And she can catch the essence of a human scene as accurately as that of an inanimate one. Here, for example, is her description of a country fair:

> I went to the fair with Ernestine and her father and mother.
> We walked through the dark quiet Lytton street under a
> night of stars towards the garish lights and music. The
> prancing excitement that Ernestine and I felt was all mixed
> up with the greasy smells from the hot-dog stand; the
> sudden light and the sudden darkness; the cacophony of
> sound; motion revolving horizontally, vertically, passing and
> repassing; drifting town and country people; darting chil-
> dren; barking dogs; all happening together, noise, flare, smell,
> motion, and the small crowds standing with upturned faces
> gazing at the picture in front of the lighted booth of Torquil
> the Lobster Boy. (p. 45)

That conveys very well the excitement that a youngster of twelve
feels at such an event. And again it does not stand alone, but is
cleverly woven into the total fabric of the novel: having been
warned by her parents to stay away from Hetty Dorval, Frankie
is "much subdued" when she leaves for Lytton, but the "prancing
excitement" of the fair gives her the courage to call again upon
the mysterious stranger.

A sensitivity to landscape and to human gatherings is not an
unusual quality in a novelist, although Mrs. Wilson's capacities
in these areas are well above average. A rarer gift which she
possesses is the ability to convey the essence of animal and
bird behaviour. *Hetty Dorval* is not as distinguished in this respect as some of her later novels, but even in it we see signs
of unusual perceptiveness. The opening paragraphs of the novel,
quoted above, reveal how accurately Mrs. Wilson observes and
records the behaviour of dogs. Here is a passage which illustrates
how she notices a variety of animal life:

> It was a lovely ride home, as you can imagine, all along
> the Lillooet road, reining off into the sage-brush if a car came
> along in a cloud of dust, and always with accustomed coun-
> try eyes roving the expanse that unfolded itself at each bend
> of the river and road, noting whose cattle those were yonder,
> the promenading hawks, in spring the bluebirds, in summer
> the ground-hogs changing suddenly from little vertical statues
> to scurrying dust-coloured vanishing points; in autumn rein-
> ing in and standing still to watch a flying crying skein of
> wild geese, sometimes a coyote at close range—quite a pretty

little beast. And then at the end of the ride the dogs barking a welcome, and Mother and Father and hugs, Maxey to be stabled and fed, and a great big supper ready. (pp. 11–12)

The details there, especially with reference to the ground-hogs, are very closely observed.

But the most striking description of animate life in *Hetty Dorval* is this account of the flight of wild geese:

> She could not see as quickly as I could that out of the north came a thin long arrow, high in the sky. Then her eyes picked up the movement of the fluid arrow rapidly approaching overhead, and the musical clamour of the wild geese came more clearly and loudly to us. The valley of the Fraser lay broad below, lit by the September afternoon, and the geese, not too high, were now nearly overhead, travelling fast. The fluid arrow was an acute angle wavering and changing, one line straggling out far behind the other. It cleft the skies, and as always I felt an exultation, an uprush within me joining that swiftly moving company and that loud music of the wild geese. As we gazed, the moving arrow of great birds passed out of sight on its known way to the south, leaving only the memory of sight and sound in the still air. We drew a long breath. (pp. 18–19)

Even if this were merely a set-piece of description, it would be highly effective, for so often the phrasing strikes us as just right: the "fluid arrow," the "musical clamour," "an acute angle wavering and changing" all reveal that Mrs. Wilson has looked and noted and found the exact word in which to record her perceptions. But the wild geese are also a symbol of Hetty Dorval, who like them longs to be free to move without encumbrance. The flight of the wild geese, indeed, becomes one of the chief thematic motifs in the novel. When Frankie is first told by her parents of Hetty's notoriety, she cites Hetty's love of wild geese "as a proof of her innocence." Later, when Frankie tells Mrs. Dorval that her parents will not let her see Hetty again, the latter says that she had thought she could trust Frankie because of their mutual love of wild geese. When they meet again in a London restaurant, Hetty reminds Frankie of "the wild geese going overhead"; and in their very last scene together Hetty recalls the flight once more.

The wild geese symbolize not only Hetty's own love of wild-
ness and freedom, but all the redeeming features of her character: like them she is a kind of spontaneous natural force, with
her own way of being. And the character of Hetty, together with
the complementary character of Frankie, constitutes the very core
of this novel. In one sense, *Hetty Dorval* is still another version
of the classic confrontation of innocence and experience. It would
almost be possible to treat the novel as an allegory, in which
Innocence meets Evil in the disguise of Beauty, is temporarily
enchanted thereby, is made wise by Parental Wisdom, and succeeds finally in cheating Evil out of another victim. But although
there is just enough of this element in the novel to make such
a summary possible, and to set up interesting analogies with
Spenser's *Faerie Queene* and Bunyan's *Pilgrim's Progress,* the
summary grossly oversimplifies the moral and psychological subtlety of the book.

III   *Thematic Patterns*

We have already mentioned that one of the chief thematic
motifs is the flight of the wild geese. The other, and slightly
more important one, is the well-known quotation from Donne's
meditations which serves as the novel's epigraph:

> No man is an Iland, intire of it selfe; every man is a peece
> of the Continent, a part of the maine; if a Clod bee washed
> away by the Sea, Europe is the lesse, as well as if a Promon-
> torie were, as well as if a Mannor of thy friends or of thine
> owne were; any mans death diminishes me, because I am
> involved in Mankinde.

This epigraph is picked up at intervals throughout the book.
When Frankie is in Cornwall, she thinks about Hetty in these
terms:

> Any positive efforts that one could discern on the part of
> Hetty were directed towards isolating herself from responsi-
> bilities to other people. She endeavoured to island herself
> in her own particular world of comfort and irresponsibility.
> ("I will *not* have my life complicated.") But "No man is an
> Iland; intire of it selfe"; said Mother's poet three hundred

years ago, and Hetty could not island herself, because we impinge on each other, we touch, we glance, we press, we touch again, we cannot escape. (p. 72)

And that last phrase, "we cannot escape," of course, calls to mind the other contrasting thematic motif, that of the wild geese —who can escape, who can leave for the south whenever instinct so directs.

The novel, in other words, seesaws between two opposed views of the human condition, between responsibility and irresponsibility, discipline and license, communalism and individualism. Swayed by her admiration for Hetty, Frankie leans to the wild goose view of life; reproved by her parents, she veers to the sense of communal responsibility. Responsibility triumphs in Frankie: when she becomes aware of the destructive influence which Hetty threatens to exercise on her Cornish friends, Rick and Molly, Frankie rejects Hetty (symbolically trying to push her out of bed). But Hetty clings throughout to the wild goose way, and Frankie cannot quite eliminate a rebellious, reluctant envy of her freedom:

> Although I had fought her and driven her off, and would fight her again if I had to and defeat her, too, she was hard to hate as I looked at her. She made a gesture of good-bye and went down the stairs. (*Mrs. Broom, to what a bleak morning you awoke all alone.*)
>
> As I watched with satisfaction Hetty going down the narrow stairs, I knew that before she had taken three steps she had forgotten me, and she had forgotten Richard. She was on her way. (p. 116)

The italicized sentence, reminding us of Hetty's callous desertion of her mother, is there to call to our minds the suffering to others which is involved in the individualist's relentless search for personal liberty. On the other hand, there is no mistaking the slightly envious tone of the last sentence: "She was on her way."

The only words that follow that sentence, which comes on the last page of the novel, are these:

Six weeks later the German Army occupied Vienna. There

arose a wall of silence around the city, through which only
faint confused sounds were sometimes heard. (p. 116)

This final paragraph makes intelligible another quotation from
Donne which occurs in the epigraph, below the Island passage:
"And makes one little room an everywhere."

The story, in its modest way, is being held up as a microcosm
of the whole human world prior to the Great War. The irresponsible individualism of Hetty Dorval, multiplied a million times,
precipitated that conflict. And since no man is an island, that
conflict destroyed not only the individualists but the communalists
as well.

The foregoing discussion, however, suggests that the novel is
much more abstractly moral than it really is. Moreover, *Hetty
Dorval* is most satisfying not on the moral but on the psychological plane. The seesaw of conflicting moral philosophies is
there, but it is not nearly as fascinating as the seesaw of conflicting personalities.

IV *Characterization*

At first reading, the most interesting character in the novel is
Hetty Dorval herself. The process by which she is gradually revealed to us through the eyes of Frankie is subtle and delicate.
At first merely a strange visitor, she comes to seem in time a
beautiful and gracious hostess, probably the innocent victim of
malicious gossip, a wicked temptress, a weak woman grasping
at happiness, and a *femme fatale*. She is elusive and chameleon-
like, and Frankie is never sure just what she really is. To the
very end she remains an enigma, disappearing for reasons which
she alone knows into the silence of war-time Vienna.

Frankie's first sight of her comes when she meets her on horse-
back, when they are both riding towards Lytton on a Saturday
afternoon. What impresses Frankie on this occasion is Hetty's
beauty, kindness, purity, and innocence; but the first crack in
this image comes a few moments later, when Mrs. Dorval uses
the word "God" as an expletive. To the child's mind, this spells
wickedness:

> I was brought shockingly to earth. I was quite used to
> hearing the men round Mr. Rossignol's stable, and other

men too, say "God" for no reason at all. And it goes without
saying that the Rev. Mr. Thompson said "God" in church,
as it were officially, and that we all sang about God with
nothing more than ordinary church-going emotion. But
never, never, in our house (except once or twice, Father) or
in Ernestine's house or at Mrs. Dunne's or in any of our
friends' houses (unless we were saying our prayers) did
people ever mention God. (p. 19)

Almost immediately afterwards comes the realization that Mrs.
Dorval is literally "two-faced":

We remained standing there and gazing at the empty sky.
Then Mrs. Dorval turned her face on me and I realized all
of a sudden that she had another face. This full face was
different from the profile I had been studying, and was
for the moment animated. Her brows, darker than her fair
hair, pointed slightly upwards in the middle in moments of
stress and became in appearance tragic, and her eyes which
were fringed with thick, short, dark lashes opened wide
and looked brilliant instead of serene. The emotion might
be caused by pain, by the beauty of flighting geese, by death,
or even by some very mild physical discomfort, but the
impact on the beholder was the same, and arresting. Ordinarily, Mrs. Dorval's full face was calm and somewhat
indolent. The purity was not there, but there was what
I later came to regard as a rather pleasing yet disturbing
sensual look, caused I think by the over-fullness of the curved
mouth, and by those same rounded high cheek-bones which
in profile looked so tender. (pp. 19–20)

When, during Frankie's first visit to Mrs. Dorval's bungalow,
the Reverend Mr. Thompson comes to call, Frankie realizes that
Hetty is also two-faced in the moral sense. She is gracious and
apparently friendly to the minister while he is there, but once
he has gone she tells her housekeeper, Mrs. Broom ("Mouse"),
that she will not have callers:

"Now Mouse," said Mrs. Dorval, "I will not be called upon.
I will not have my life complicated here . . . people coming
in like this! I do not propose to spend my time paying attention to all kinds of people. You know perfectly well that I

can't have people running in, and you must stop it." (It
might have been Mrs. Broom's fault.) "All I ask of anybody
is to be left alone and not be interfered with. I'm sure I
always leave people quite alone and interfere with nobody." (p. 26)

Frankie leaves this first interview with Mrs. Dorval with mixed
feelings. Her beauty of face and voice (Mrs. Dorval sings for
Frankie after the minister has left) charms the girl: "As for me,
a country child, I had come under a very fancy kind of spell,
near to infatuation." (p. 27) And yet she cannot help feeling
that "there was something somewhere that was not quite right,"
particularly when Mrs. Dorval's last admonition to her is to
keep the visit secret:

> Whatever she had asked me, then, I would have agreed to
> do, and this seemed a small thing to promise, so I did. But
> it passed through my mind that it would be a funny thing
> if I came to this house and my mother couldn't come, that
> is, even if she wanted to. But I was only twelve, and was
> under a novel spell of beauty and singing and the excite-
> ment of a charm that was new, and I went away almost
> in a trance. (p. 27)

We have followed the development of Hetty Dorval's character far enough to make clear the subtle and delicate way in
which it is managed. What makes the process doubly interesting
is the interplay of Frankie's character with that of Hetty: it is
not so much what Hetty *is* that intrigues us, as what she appears
to be to the innocent but perceptive beholder. Frankie serves
the function in this novel of the innocent eye in whose gaze everything has its own wonder and mystery of being. Indeed on a
second reading of the novel one is apt to find Frankie's character
even more intriguing than that of Hetty. Whereas the development in Hetty's character is only the growing realization of what
has actually been there all along, Frankie's character does change
as the novel progresses. At the beginning she is a completely
innocent and ignorant country girl of twelve, so naive that a
visit to the station to watch a train come in is an event; by the
end of the novel she is a young woman of nineteen who has been
to school in Vancouver and in England, who has lived in London
and Paris, and who is sophisticated enough to entertain her

friends in a fashionable London restaurant. But the change is not
merely this relatively commonplace one, from childish naiveté to
adult sophistication. Frankie's innocence is not quite spoiled but
it is certainly strained by her relationship with Hetty. Frankie
indeed takes on some of the characteristics of the company she
keeps. She hides her visits to Hetty from her parents; on one
occasion she plays the part of a peeping Tom, spying through
Hetty's window; and in the last scene of the novel it is suggested
that Frankie has become almost as selfish and self-indulgent as
Hetty. In words which inevitably recall Mrs. Dorval's speech to
Mrs. Broom after the minister's visit, Frankie says to Hetty:

> "I don't want you here again! You muddle up my life too
> much. Please, Hetty, look after your own affairs but keep
> away from me. I've got my own life to live and I don't want
> ever to see you again—*ever*." (p. 114)

As if to underline the similarity of attitude, Mrs. Wilson has
Hetty reply:

> "I understand *exactly*. I feel for you. It is preposterous the
> way other people clutter up and complicate one's life. It is
> my own phobia, Frankie, and I understand you . . . so well."
> (p. 114).

V *Style and Tone*

The style of *Hetty Dorval*, apart from a few passages of brilliant
landscape description, is simple and unobtrusive. There are very
few metaphors and similes, but the few that do occur are characteristic of Mrs. Wilson in that they draw analogies between
human and non-human beings. Frankie thinks of herself as a
goldfish: "But I lived in a glass goldfish bowl where the behaviour
of each fish was visible to all the other fishes, and also to grown-
up people outside and in the vicinity of the glass bowl." (p. 29)
Hetty appears to Frankie as a cat:

> Hetty Dorval was a human cat in some ways, and yet cats
> have sometimes malice, and they sharpen their claws. But
> Hetty had no malice. She was as incapable of bearing malice
> as of bearing resentment. She simply shed people, and I only
> once caught a glimpse of her claws. (p. 30)

A group of Indians at the fair are compared to birds: "The Indians, in small groups, moved always together, as by some inner
self-protective compulsion, like certain birds, with their own
particular kind of awareness." (p. 45)

The most outstanding characteristic of the novel's style is its
clever modulation of tone. Sometimes the modulation is so subtle
as to be scarcely noticeable, as in this scene where the Reverend
Mr. Thompson has called upon Hetty at her bungalow:

> "Then you are English," continued Mr. Thompson.
> "Well . . . no," said Mrs. Dorval.
> "Is your husband English? Or I should say, was your home
> there?"
> "No," said Mrs. Dorval.
> There was a pause.
> "I hope your husband will be able to join you here," said
> Mr. Thompson.
> "Oh, I *do* hope so," said Mrs. Dorval. She spoke little but
> her words did not come snubbingly as Mrs. Broom's would
> have done, but gently.
> "A reader, I see," said Mr. Thompson.
> "Yes," said Mrs. Dorval.
> Mr. Thompson got up and evidently went over to the
> bookshelves where I had seen a lot of yellowish paper books.
> "Ah, you read French!"
> "Yes, I read French."
> "I should like you to meet my wife. She would be very
> glad to call upon you, she is a reader too."
> "Call?" said Mrs. Dorval vaguely and sweetly. "Oh, not
> call, you have no idea . . . Oh, you are so kind, but at
> present . . ." and she looked at Mr. Thompson.
> Mr. Thompson murmured something about "restored
> health" and then after a little more unsatisfactory conversa-
> tion, said what I had been waiting for him to say, "And
> now shall we have a word of prayer?"
> "Oh," breathed Mrs. Dorval, sitting motionless. (pp. 23–
> 24)

Almost every sentence in that scene is ambiguous and ironic,
and we are invited to react to each remark and action in three
ways at once—to sympathize with the curiosity, shock, and simple

piety of the minister, to sense Mrs. Dorval's desire to fend the
minister off and yet not truly offend him, and at the same time
to respond to the scene with all of Frankie's bewilderment.
There is an intricate interplay of piety, sophisticated boredom,
and childish innocence, so that what seems at first glance so
simple a style of utterance is actually functioning in a very
complex manner indeed.

Sometimes the modulation of tone is more obvious. In the
last scene, Hetty spends the night in Frankie's room, and goes
to sleep in her bed. As she looks at the sleeping Hetty, Frankie is
once more impressed with her tender innocence, and feels for
her a rich compassion:

> There is that in sleep which reduces us all to one common
> denominator of helplessness and vulnerable humanity. The
> soft rise and fall of the unconscious sleeper's breast is a
> miracle. It is a binding symbol of our humanity. The child
> in the lost attitude of sleep is all children, everywhere, in
> all time. A sleeping human being is all people, sleeping,
> everywhere since time began. There is that in the sleeper
> that arrests one, pitying, and that makes us all the same.
> The rise and the fall of the frail envelope of skin that con-
> tains the microcosm of wonder, is the touching sign. If one
> had an enemy, and if one saw that enemy sleeping, one
> might be dangerously moved in pity of spirit by what lies
> there, unconscious. I looked at Hetty, sleeping; but that did
> not prevent me from prodding her and saying, "Hetty, *move*
> over, I've got to get to sleep!" There was a murmur, "Oh,
> *poor* Frankie," and she moved luxuriously nearer to her edge
> of the bed and I lay down and turned off the light. (pp.
> 111–12)

Just as the passage is threatening to become sentimental, Mrs.
Wilson modulates the tone to one of natural human irritation,
and the scene is saved.

But the passage just quoted may also serve to illustrate another feature of Mrs. Wilson's style, and this is a less laudable
one. She is rather too prone to adopt the old-fashioned device
of authorial comment, to intrude into the flow of her narrative
little chunks of personal philosophy. Usually there is a flavour
of irony in these remarks which helps to make them palatable,
but they do sometimes offend.

Hetty Dorval is a work of apprenticeship, and cannot compare in depth of thought and complexity of technique with Mrs. Wilson's later novels. Nevertheless, it is a novel of genuine charm. For all its apparent simplicity, it offers us contrasting views of the human condition and embodies these attitudes in two intriguing characters. In addition, it contains descriptions of the fauna, flora and landscape of British Columbia which cleverly combine accuracy with suggestiveness. Its unassuming, delicately modulated tone forms a fitting prelude to Mrs. Wilson's career as a novelist.

CHAPTER 4

The Innocent Traveller (1949)

THE *Innocent Traveller* is the longest and most complex of
Ethel Wilson's novels; it is also the most personal, the most
consciously Canadian, and the most completely satisfying. It is
the most personal in that it is a thinly disguised history of her
own family, and one of the characters in the novel—Rose—is
almost certainly Mrs. Wilson herself; the most consciously Canadian in that she gives at length the reaction to Canada of her
relatives and describes in detail the scenery of Canada from
coast to coast; the most completely satisfying in that style, theme,
character, setting, imagery, and symbols are beautifully integrated. But it is also a very complex novel, although its complexity, as is usual in Mrs. Wilson's work, lies beneath a decep-
tively simple surface.

Since the novel is a complex one, the critic must attempt to
disentangle the many strands that are cunningly woven into its
single fabric. It seems to me that its pattern can best be seen as a
series of concentric circles. At the very centre is Topaz Edgeworth, "the innocent traveller," and if one focuses on her, it
becomes a novel of character, or a fictionalized biography. In
the first circle around Topaz are her relatives, the large and
diverse Edgeworth family, and at this level the novel is a family
saga. The next circle is formed by the changing society, first
English and then Canadian, in which Topaz and her family
function; and the detailed attention which is devoted to social
change gives the novel the quality of a chronicle. The novel also
has some elements of the travelogue, for a good deal of it is
devoted to the scenic description of Staffordshire, parts of
Europe, and, especially, Canada and Vancouver. Beyond that
again is the circle of interlinked imagery and symbolism, which

gives to the novel many of the qualities of an elegiac poem.
Finally, one may see the novel as a parable of the relations be-
tween Man and Nature, Innocence and Experience, Time and
Eternity, Paganism and Christianity, Life and Death.

I *Characterization: Topaz*

On the most obvious level, *The Innocent Traveller* is the life
story of Topaz Edgeworth, who is a little girl of three or so
living in the Staffordshire town of Ware when the novel opens,
and an old woman of a hundred when she dies in Vancouver
at the novel's close. "Topaz" as a mineral is defined by the
Shorter Oxford English Dictionary as a "fluosilicate of aluminium,
transparent and lustrous, yellow, white, pale blue or pale green,"
and Topaz as a character is indeed a hard, bright, multi-coloured
being. She is introduced to us first as one "who could not be
squelched,"[1] who is "as innocent as a poached egg," and she
retains this dual quality of toughness and innocence to the end
of her long life. Her innocence, however, is a more complex
affair than might be imagined: it is certainly not to be confused
with ignorance, because eventually Topaz becomes a woman of
considerable education and sophistication; nor, on the other
hand, is it to be confused with sanctity, a quality her sister Annie
possesses but Topaz never. Nor is her innocence a freedom from
all faults, for Topaz has many faults: she is "anxious to be
noticed" (p. 2), rebellious, aggravating, irascible, garrulous,
bumptious, idle, "congenitally lacking in any private or inner
life" (p. 61), irreverent, "she had no reticence," (p. 64) oblivious
to the subtler forms of human relationship, irresponsible, bad-
mannered (for she "had the gift of belching delicately, when
and where and as often as she chose." [p. 163]), impatient, de-
ficient in imagination ("Aunt Topaz, who had almost no imagination at all, read the [casualty] lists also, and to her the names
were not people but numbers," [p. 216]), unobservant of public
events and of nature's beauty. Her innocence seems to consist
of a fresh, unabashed, unconventional, enthusiastic and gay response to life. Whatever her faults, she has the triumphant virtue
of never being bored or jaded.

Topaz always confronts experience with a genuine and individual enthusiasm. "Only the small and irascible Topaz was an

individual from the time she uttered her first sentence . . . until
that day nearly a century later when, still speaking clearly, she
died." (p. 15) She sparkles, she is lively, she is volatile and she
is extroverted. Although her life is uneventful from a conventional point of view, it does not seem so to her. From her school-
mistress, a lover of Greek civilization, she has picked up the
pagan spirit of eager enjoyment of the here and now. "Topaz
loved the sound of music. . . . She enjoyed music as she enjoyed
food, with pleasure, but without passion, like a warbling unim-
portant bird." (pp. 44–45) She is not "particularly useful" but
she is "unquenchably gay." (p. 59) She sets out on any adventure
full of joy and anticipation, and she is not inhibited by social
conventions: it does not at all bother her that her skirts fly up
(to the admiration of watching Frenchmen) as she climbs the
Eiffel Tower—but it bothers her brother John exceedingly. When
she visits the Sistine Chapel, she lies on her back the better to
view Michelangelo's ceiling—in spite of the fact that she is
then a woman of forty-five.

Topaz' innocence is a kind of naturalness which refuses to
make conventional distinctions. "Topaz rejoiced too openly, she
had no reticence; she did not seem to know the right people from
the wrong people." (p. 64) When an amorous Frenchman in
Lyons talks to her beside her open bedroom door and puts his
hand on her arm, Topaz merely dusts him off and goes on talking
"with her usual eager vivacity." (p. 65) She has really nothing
to fear, for she is "armed with all her gay purity." (p. 66) Nor
has she any need of artificial stimulants: she is "sufficiently
intoxicated by nature without drinking wine." (p. 66) The result
is that all her journeys are "packed with adventure and remi-
niscence." (p. 68) "The world blossomed daily into incident;
and so the years passed too quickly." (p. 68) At forty-five she
is "still in her light-hearted minority" (p. 71); at forty-eight
she is still "a young girl (p. 74); at fifty she is "only a girl grown
old, however much strangers might take her for a woman." (p. 87)
Whatever her age, whatever her circumstances, she talks in-
cessantly: "If no human ears were within range, she talked to
animals or to birds. . . . She disliked silence. Silence existed only
to be broken." (p. 75)

But if Topaz cares nothing for convention, she does have her
loyalties:

Into her majority and for ever, Topaz took her three loyalties. Not religion, although she had an indigenous faith in God, for Topaz might well have been (and perhaps she had been) a heavy-footed Bacchante, a milder Maenad with satin white skin, dancing heavily and happily, excited before the flickering shrine, carefree among the olive trees, calling to the other boys and girls; not patriotism, although she loved her country; not love for a man—William Sandbach had become only a still interesting object seen from afar. But the Royal Family moved through her life with banners streaming. Mr. Gladstone stood for ever four-square in his integrity ("Yes, I shook his hand, I heard his wonderful voice—like an organ it was . . .") and through his spell she adhered in a wishy-washy way to the Liberal Party. And now her loyalty to her father lived as a loving memory—or perhaps it expanded, to include the person of her little eldest sister. (pp. 89–90)

These loyalties to tradition, however, do not inhibit her from making a fresh response to the New World. Once en route to Canada, "she turned readily to the West and faced a fresh free life which she was eager to enjoy." (p. 92) She is forever looking to the future, for all her love of the past:

Her sister Topaz, taking down addresses, promising visits, recklessly giving invitations, running round to people's cabins, lending books, returning scarves, impeding stewards, collecting autographs at parties, hardly had time to regret the end of the journey across the famous Atlantic Ocean, in the anticipation of something imminent, new, and rare. (p. 97)

Her combined innocence and toughness allow her to go through life as gaily as a water-glider skims the surface of a pool:

Topaz got on the train with practically nothing at all. She travelled light. A native toughness enabled her to carry her few strong loyalties without inconvenience to herself, but for the rest, the joy of living was daily renewed in her and was seldom checked by things, people, or events. This joy, which was concerned only with the veriest surface of material and psychic being, allowed her to amuse herself like

> those "water-gliders" which we see in summer running about
> on the top of pleasant weed-fringed pools. (p. 103)

And so she can enjoy, and not in anyway be damaged by, a conversation with the men in the train's smoking room.

Topaz' enthusiasm for life finds plenty of scope in the new
province of British Columbia:

> Topaz had at last reached open country. British Columbia
> stretched before her, exciting her with its mountains, its
> forests, the Pacific Ocean, the new little frontier town, and
> all the new people. Here was no time limit, no fortnight's
> holiday. Here she had come to live; and, drawing long
> breaths of the opulent air, she began to run about, and
> dance for joy, exclaiming, all through the open country. (p.
> 122)

She plunges into the pursuit of new friends, buys a noble but
intractable English bicycle, becomes an ardent if erratic shopper,
joins innumerable clubs and societies—only to relinquish her
offices in them once they begin to inhibit her freedom. She
finds that there are conventions and pettiness even in the new
society, however, and one of her great moments comes when she
defends a woman who is falsely accused of having rested in the
arms of a Negro swimming instructor down at English Bay.
It is this episode which prompts her niece Rachel to make one of
the most explicit statements about one facet of Topaz' innocence:
her complete lack of malice. Rachel says, "I have never heard you
say an unkind thing about anyone. I have never heard you cast
an aspersion on anyone. I really believe you are one of the few
people who think no evil." (p. 157)

Another facet of Topaz' innocence is that she is almost impossible to shock, and difficult to frighten. When she comes upon
a group of young men bathing in the nude she bends down to see
them better and exclaims, "Nothing on! Very pleasant, I'm
sure!" (p. 180) One memorable night, however, she *is* frightened
—when she decides to sleep outside on the verandah at the family
cottage and hears strange noises in the night. In a passage
somewhat reminiscent of the "panic and emptiness" sequences in
E. M. Forster's *Howard's End*, Mrs. Wilson writes:

Again the descending notes of the flute, and a groan, dropping into the night.

Inside the white satin body of Topaz—satin white until the day of her death—there opened a dark unknown flower of fear. Slowly it opened, and through the orifice of this flower fear poured into the darkness. Her whole body dissolved listening into fear which flowed into the terrible enclosing night. She, all alone, became only a frightened part of the listening elements.

The high sweet sound continued again into a groan. She could not tell whether the fluting came now at regular intervals. It came. It came. It was light but clear and stronger than the silence into which it fell. "Oh God Our Help. Oh God Our Help," said a residuum of Topaz blindly. She could not remember anything more to say. But the sweet sound came again, undefeated and unperturbed by the Holy Name. *Then I must go or I am lost this is Panic I have heard it now at any moment I shall see him close in the darkness I shall feel his breath!* And she sprang up, not knowing what she did and seized soft quilt and Grandfather's shawl, and stumbling, trailing, upsetting, she found the door. She wrenched the door open and rushed in. She shut the door and locked it. (p. 193)

Such fear, however, is temporary. Topaz triumphs over more really forbidding circumstances. When she is an old woman of seventy-five and her elder sister Annie and her niece Rachel, who have been her companions and guardians for years, die and leave her virtually on her own resources, she does not despair but rather enters her apotheosis:

Aunty lay in her last phoenix fire of sorrow. She did not know that it was a phoenix fire which consumed her, and that, in her own remarkable way, she would arise from this fire and become more resilient, more strong, impervious to grief and even to love, and that now, at the age of seventy-five, she was entering into her own little apotheosis, and nothing mortal, not even death itself, would be able to move her or hurt her any more. (p. 225)

In the last quarter century of her life she has some of her

most exciting experiences: she has an interview with Queen Mary at Buckingham Palace, declares that she is a colonial and is proud of it, acquires for the first time her own apartment, and rules her shrinking but perpetually interesting world like an empress. Her fingers are now crooked, but she is never ill, and she still, at the age of ninety, "dearly loves a party." (p. 244) In fact life to her has become a party at which she is the guest of honour. She can boast "Out to dinner and ME ninety-three" (p. 246) and exclaim "WHAT, NO MEN? I thought we were going to have a right good time!" (p. 247) In her nineties she still has her loyalties and her unconcern for convention: hence she causes quite a commotion in the lobby of the Empress Hotel in Victoria by bowing ceremoniously to the portraits of the King and Queen. Her very obliviousness to the great destructive forces forms a protection against them:

> In the evening while the sea-gulls fly westwards with lazy purposeful flight, and great and terrible events are massed by Time and Plan upon the slow-moving curtain, Aunt Topaz gathers the rattling newspaper together and with her embroidery scissors cuts out a picture of the King and Queen, an account of a wedding, and an advertisement for garlic pearls because they sound so odd. She may send for these pearls some day. She puts the newspaper cuttings into a large overfull box with a red plush cover on which some sea-shells still remain. She is very old. She will soon be a hundred. (p. 263)

Even against Death she is invincible, for she has no fear of it:

> Because Great-Aunt Topaz is a hundred years old and is still little Topaz Edgeworth with a strong infusion of *grande dame*, she is invincible. Small and great lapses from convention do not dismay her. . . . she is impatient of illness but not at all dismayed by death, which can now almost be heard approaching, it is so near. (p. 271)

All that she feels, as death approaches, is a slight restlessness to be gone:

> Her world continues to shrink. It is a bed; it is a cup of

milk; it is a voice which she essays to greet with customary friendliness. Her memories have flowed away. Wherever can they be? Only habit remains.

Her world has closed down to a point; it is a point of departure. She is restless and ill at ease. (p. 274)

When she dies, she is like a bird escaping from a cage rather than a bird being trapped:

Topaz is dying, there is no doubt of that. She—gay, volatile, one hundred years old, the last of her generation, long delayed—is uneasy. She is very restless. She shows no fear and yet she seems to be in some kind of anguish. Plainly she is awaiting something, an affirmation or release. What is that she is saying? She wants to go, she says. She is being prevented. The poor volatile bird.

"Let me go immediately . . . immediately . . ." she murmurs in her imperious way. "A hundred years . . . I shall be late . . . me, the youngest." Then the small face lightens. "Quick, get me some fresh lace for me head, someone! I'm going to die, I do declare!" Evidently she is pleased and confident. What an adventure, to be sure!

Away she went. Now she is a memory, a gossamer. (p. 275)

The desire to ensure that Aunt Topaz would linger in people's memories was probably the prime motive leading Ethel Wilson to write this book. She prefaces the novel with these lines from Donne:

And as if on a stream I fixe mine eye,
That drop, which I looked on, is presently
Pusht with more waters from my sight, and gone.

And in the course of the novel she has a young scion of the family reflect as follows:

My Great-Grandmother . . . needs no memorial. There are forty of us—why there must be over fifty of us now!—Canadians, up and down the country, who have issued from her or from her issue, and for better or worse we are her memorial. And my Great-Aunt Rachel, whom I just remember, needs no memorial either, because there are still people who knew her and honoured her quite a lot, and anyway, a person like my Great-Aunt Rachel has her own memorial. But Great-Great-Aunt Topaz, who outlived these two, and outlived all her generation, and many of the next generation, and some of the next generation, and who defied these generations in her later days—don't I remember her!—she has gone; there is no mark of her that I know, no more than the dimpling of the water caused by the wind a few minutes ago. She is only a line on granite, "Sister of the Above." Yet she lived a hundred years, and is not long dead. Already she is seldom mentioned, and when we meet together as we sometimes do, all so busy, all so occupied, perhaps no one remembers, until afterwards, to mention her name. And the little ones will not even know her name. It is really a shame . . . that one can live a hundred years with gusto, and be happy, and agitate the stream, and pass at once out of memory. (pp. 104–5)

It is a tribute to Mrs. Wilson's skill that Aunt Topaz does haunt the memory once this book has been read. Although her life-story is comparatively uneventful, and although she has none of the conventional attributes of heroism, we feel her death as a moving personal loss. As a piece of characterization, in other words, the book is a triumph. By subtle little strokes, applied with great patience and tact, Mrs. Wilson has contrived to paint a portrait which glows with life and truth.

II   *The Edgeworth Family*

The Innocent Traveller, however, is not only a biography of Aunt Topaz, it is also a saga of the Edgeworth family. Seldom has a novel succeeded in making its readers so conscious of family relationships, family loyalties and rivalries, as does this one. It opens with the family at dinner and it ends with the family at Topaz' funeral. The novel is punctuated with family occasions: births, marriages, parties, dinners, birthdays, deaths, funerals, departures, arrivals, and reunions. The word "family" appears on almost every page, and family names—Father, Mother, Aunt, Uncle, Grandfather, Grandmother, Great Aunt, Great Great Uncle—proliferate as the story proceeds. For the Edgeworths, a sense of membership in the family precedes a sense of individuality:

> So strong was the woven fabric of their large domestic life
> that the Edgeworth family were first of all members one of
> another, and next, each became aware of his own indi-
> viduality. They were sons, daughters, sisters, and brothers
> before they were people. They rapidly became cousins,
> nieces, and nephews. Also uncles and aunts. Quickly one
> child, slowly another, apprehended its own condition as a
> person. (p. 15)

We get interesting reminders of the rules of decorum that
prevailed in families in Victorian times:

> In orderly families, such as the Edgeworths', Father and
> Mother, flanked and separated down a fairly long table by
> a double row of children, might consider themselves to be
> practically alone. At the Edgeworth table no child, save one
> [the exception, of course, is Topaz] raised his or her voice
> unless addressed. All, save one, behaved with astonishing
> decorum, while Father and Mother carried on their own
> Olympian conversations. The six remaining sons and daugh-
> ters were as nearly inaudible as six normal children could
> be except for Topaz, who could not keep silent (how should
> she, who talked persistently for over ninety-seven years?),
> and was often admonished by both parents, and sometimes
> had to be sent from the table because she was too bumptious;
> and Topaz annoyed only in the same way that a fly annoys.
> Father and Mother, being alone then, except for at least
> eight other people in the room counting Emma and Cook or
> Betsy, spoke freely to each other and settled much of their
> domestic business at the table. (p. 23)

Later on, we see the family in the family pew at church, and
engaged in family prayer.

Individualist as Topaz is, even she has an overpowering sense
of her place in the family:

> For, speaking clearly, the words she said as she died were,
> "Me, the youngest!" and although the last of her generation
> had twenty years ago departed, her life was still tied to her

powerful assembled family which had slipped one by one
with acceptance or amazement through the strangely moving
curtain of Time into another place. (p. 16; cf. p. 275)

Her age and status are measured in family terms: "Topaz had
already become Aunt Topaz, and was now on her way to being
Great-Aunt Topaz, without noticing it at all." (p. 72)

For the most part, the family is portrayed favourably, as a
barrier against the outside world, against Time and Death (this
chronicle is a succession of deaths in the family—but the family,
although it is dispersed at the end, has survived and will survive.) But the weaknesses of the family are not ignored. There
is a certain smugness and insensitivity involved in family intro-
version:

> Father and the Stepmother and their biddable lively daugh-
> ter Topaz now lived together with serenity and much quiet
> dignity, comfortably served and attended, removed by trees
> and garden from the busy thoroughfare, and by lack of
> imagination from the bitter realities of their world, to which,
> however, Mr. Charles Dickens and others had begun to call
> their attention. (p. 40)

And there are times when the closeness of the family atmosphere
becomes irritating and almost stifling: the whole of Chapter
XVIII, entitled "Rather Close in the Sitting-Room" is devoted
to the illustration of this fact.

The members of the family provide a brilliant group of secondary characters, and make excellent foils for Topaz. None of
them are stereotypes. Topaz' Father, for example, is in many
ways the typical Victorian *pater familias*, stern, dignified,
bearded, aloof, magisterial. His values are the assured values of
his century:

> Great-Grandfather Edgeworth sat in the garden in the sun-
> shine. A white handkerchief covered his face. Puff in, puff
> out, puff in, puff out. The white handkerchief, neatly secured
> under his round black skull-cap, rose and fell with the blasts
> from his wide ingenuous nostrils. Behind the concealing and
> expressionless handkerchief was the noble face of the sleep-
> ing old man. Happy, happy old man. He sat there, sleeping
> in security in the sunshine. His world was a good world. His

Queen was a good Queen. His country was a good country. His business was good. His health was good. His family was a good family and God was good. All this goodness flowed together in this strong and gentle old man. He had served his community well. He had never turned aside from recognized Duty. He had known consolable grief and inevitable worry, but not much grief and not much worry, and no doubts. None. God? God, invisible but real, was obscured from him only by the lofty and so often clouded English skies, but with spiritual eyes Great-Grandfather Edgeworth beheld his Maker. (pp. 72–73)

But when, at the age of ninety, twice a widower, he proposes marriage to two old ladies in turn in one afternoon, he breaks from the stereotype and becomes triumphantly an individual. The chapter retailing these proposals, Chapter IX, "Nuts and Figs," is one of the most brilliantly amusing in the book.

Apart from Father, the three most interesting and fully developed members of the family are Topaz' elder sister Annie, Annie's daughter and Topaz' niece Rachel, and Topaz' grandniece, Rose. Whereas Topaz is volatile and erratic, these three of her close associates are dependable and stable.

Annie's anchor is religion: "wherever she might go, in all circumstances and places, the Grandmother was at home, because she carried heaven in her heart and face." (p. 91) When she steps on the train to cross Canada to Vancouver, we are told that she took with her "her powerful spiritual awareness and lasting gentle domination, and her other-worldliness." (pp. 102–3). She is a kind of saint:

> Dr. Carboy read from the Word. The Grandmother leaned forward. Her soft eyes were upon him. She listened with her ears and with her soft eyes and with her luminous countenance and with the other-worldliness and selflessness and consecration that made her a saint, as if she had never heard the familiar holy words before. (pp. 174–75)

She has "a natural radiance" that spreads "straight to God" (p. 177) and " Communion with God, a great and infinitely loving Father" is "the great fact of Grannie's life." (p. 209) It is wholly

appropriate that her last words should be *"I am very thankful,
love. God bless you always, Rachel."* (p. 220)

Rachel is not so much saintly as dutiful. When Annie is described as taking on to the Canadian train her powerful spiritual
awareness, we are told of Rachel:

> Her daughter Rachel took all her anxieties, her fierce sense of
> duty, her integrity, and a great deal of practical irritable
> commonsense which, although hampered as yet by inexperi-
> ence, could readily be applied in nearly all circumstances
> which affected those who were in her charge at any place
> or time. Of herself, Rachel never had time to think, and so
> in her the habit of anxious responsibility to which she was
> disposed had taken root and was to grow. It became as a
> beech tree, and, under its fine shade, unessential flowers of
> ease and frivolity were apt not to flourish, and luxury could
> not grow where the beech leaves fell. (p. 103)

Rachel is the practical one, the Martha to Annie's Mary, who
makes of the family home a "small, warm, and well-conducted
world." (p. 161)

> It was Rachel who, with a self-less filial piety, and sometimes
> with sharp admonishings, was still her mother's proud serv-
> ant. It was Rachel who was the only subduer of the efferves-
> cent Aunt Topaz. It was Rachel who had cared for her
> younger unmarried brother Andrew. It was Rachel who
> looked after her orphaned niece Rose, and made her hair
> shine, and disciplined her, and loved her. It was Rachel who
> controlled the wily and violent Chinese cook, Yow. And it
> was Rachel who was regarded by the family as the responsi-
> ble person in her wonted place. And for what reward did
> Rachel spend her days? For no reward other than the ful-
> fillment of her own fierce integrity and sense of order, and
> the confidence and placid affection of her family. (p. 161)

But for all her practical commonsense, Rachel is a lover of beauty,
albeit an undemonstrative one:

> There was within Rachel a virgin well into which beauty
> silently seeped. She could receive the beauty of the morning
> without speaking. She did not have to transmute this beauty

into conversation. So, now, she did not need to say to her mother, "Look, the smooth bark of the arbutus tree is like copper in the sunshine, isn't it? See how the draped branches of the cedars wave seriously! Listen to 'the innumerable laughter of the sea'!" But she turned to her mother, content, and cried in her anxious way, "Mother, what *are* you doing! Come, Anty, let us move Mother's chair out of the sun!" (p. 186)

And it is the quiet, dutiful Rachel, ironically enough, whose life is taken in such tragic circumstances that we are never told what they were:

It was about two months after their return to England that the dreadful event—too tragical to contemplate— occurred which took the life of Rachel with great suffering, and spared Aunt Topaz. The impossible had happened. Rachel had left her and was dead. (p. 225)

The youngest member of the family to play a significant role in the novel, Annie's grand-daughter Rose, seems to be modelled on Ethel Wilson herself: like Mrs. Wilson, she is left an orphan in South Africa at an early age, spends a short period of time with relatives in England, and is shipped out to Vancouver to be brought up by her grandmother and her aunt and great-aunt. Rose has Rachel's practical commonsense along with some of Topaz' gaiety. She is less volatile than Topaz—"she had already begun to lose the habit of blurting everything out, and had begun to consider" (p. 132)—but more deeply emotional. When she hears the revivalist preacher exhorting those to stand up who have a Dear One in the Promised Land, her heart is ready to burst, and she stands up no less than three times—for her father, her mother, and her baby brother. But for all her emotional sensitivity, she is "earth-bound" and "quick to detect the least scent of hypocrisy or of self-awareness." (p. 175) She resembles Topaz in her individualism: she will not allow herself to be overpowered by her dominant relatives:

But on this evening Rose got up from Family Prayer in the sitting-room after dinner in a haughty and irritable frame of mind. She was aware that the veil of her irritation hung between herself and her Maker, but she clung to her veil and wrapped it round her in defence against her Grandmother's piety, the Great-Aunt's impervious loquacity, and the domination of Aunt Rachel. (p. 200)

And she escapes from her elderly female relatives to read a sensual novel about Africa in the sanctum of her bedroom. Later she marries, and still later shocks Topaz by wearing a skimpy tennis dress and smoking cigarettes; but she is at Topaz's funeral, a faithful Edgeworth to the last.

Loosely associated with the family are the family servants, friends, and ministers of the congregations in which the family worships. The portraits of some of these characters are almost as lively as those of the actual members of the family. Yow, the Chinese cook in the Vancouver household, for example, is a strange mixture of kindly fidelity, selfish cunning, and coarse brutality. To Annie he is good and kind, but he insists on preparing meals at the times that suit his rather than the ladies' convenience; he scares the ladies by pretending that he is going to put a snake in their stew; and he gambles every evening in Vancouver's Chinatown. He bullies the ladies and yet in some respects conforms to their wishes:

They always had dinner earlier than they wanted to because Yow, whose domination had increased over all these years, wished to get out. When he got out he walked with his swaggering gait straight to Vancouver Chinatown and shed his cloak of West End respectability. He belonged to a very fast set. He became deeply and darkly a Chinese gambler. This occurred every night of the week, but his nicest and most gambling day was Sunday when he got out very early. Yow looked like a dangerous criminal, and later in life he had, unfortunately, to go to prison. No one knew what his early life had been. He was in some ways a very bad and unscrupulous man, but during the day-time he guarded the interests of his blameless household of ladies in a bullying and efficient way. Such is the power of goodness, that Yow (who was quite the wickedest person that the Grandmother had ever seen, only she did not know this) revered the Grandmother deeply. Each morning and evening this scoundrel continued to "come in" to Family Prayer, and as the little Grandmother knelt and raised her earnest and

tremulous petitions to the Lord, he also knelt without either
compulsion or contempt. When they all arose from their
knees, Yow swaggered out of the room in a more bullying
manner than usual, probably in order to re-establish himself
in his own esteem, and also in order to reimpose himself on
his ladies. (pp. 196-97)

But when Rose resists his authority by spitting on the iron to
test its readiness to press her silk blouses, he shows himself a
terrifying figure:

Defiantly she would spit upon the iron. But Yow had two
dreadful punishments for her. One was that he would pull
his loose eyelids away from his eyes, above and below, ex-
posing large unpleasant red areas. Then he would roll his
bloodshot eyes in all directions apparently independent of
each other. As in any case he was violent of face, this was
formidable, but somehow Rose could not help gazing upon
him. She had to look. Yow did another thing. With a quick
flick of his fingers he turned both eyelids inside out, and
advanced into the little laundry with what looked like two
great gobs of raw meat hanging where his eyes should be.
(p. 199)

As an example of the brevity and yet the precision with which
Mrs. Wilson sketches in portraits of friends of the family, here is
Mrs. Grimwade, one of the two elderly ladies to whom Great-
Grandfather Edgeworth proposed marriage on that memorable
afternoon:

Mrs. Grimwade now sat erect by the fire, her feet on a
hassock, her black silk skirt lifted a little, disclosing a pha-
lanx of petticoats above her slippers. Mrs. Grimwade always
raised her skirt as she sat by the fire, which at home was
always a very small fire, believing that heat was bad for
silk. So severe were Mrs. Grimwade's cerements of black,
and so forbidding and lined and yellow was her face, that
the grey and wiry ringlets that hung down each side of her
face seemed to mock the aged features they adorned. (p. 77)

Of the ministerial portraits, perhaps this of the revivalist

preacher who persuades Rose to get up three times to lament her
Dear Ones in the Promised Land is the most striking:

> So now here was the Rev. Elmer Pratt, full of zeal, swarthy,
> black-visaged, and violent of feature. Beneath his black hair
> shone his bright black eyes. Beneath his bright black eyes
> jutted his large nose. Beneath his large nose sprang and
> flourished his magnificent black moustaches. Beneath his
> vigorous chin rose up his high and stiff white collar, with a
> splendid white four-in-hand tie. The face, coarse and vigor-
> ous, was perpetually at war with the sanctity of the starched
> white collar and tie beneath. He used strange words. Rose,
> accustomed to the suave tones of her native England, was
> constantly amazed at the flat and grating voice of the Rev.
> Elmer Pratt. Whereas the ministers of the Gospel to whom
> she had listened Sunday by Sunday since infancy spoke
> gently of the love of God, the Rev. Elmer Pratt thundered
> about brothels. She supposed that brothels were places where
> broth was made and decided that the broth must be very
> bad or the Rev. Elmer Pratt would not be so angry. He also
> spoke frequently about "foaming out your shame upon your
> city streets" (see Hosea), in a way that made her feel per-
> sonally responsible, and she could only conclude that he had
> reference to the nasty habit of spitting that she had noticed
> and disliked among men in the streets of this little western
> town. There seemed to be no other explanation. Many strange
> things were uttered by the Rev. Elmer Pratt, and little of it
> did Rose understand. But once his sermons of wrath and de-
> nunciation were over, he became a human and kindly being.
> (p. 137)

III *Social History*

It is just this kind of accurate observation that makes *The Innocent Traveller* such a fascinating social chronicle. Mrs. Wilson
conducts us from Staffordshire in the mid-nineteenth century to
British Columbia in the mid-twentieth, and by noticing the little
details of dress, social behaviour, domestic arrangement, and
means of travel she makes every stage of the process seem real.
There are almost no set-pieces of social comment or history—the

description of Great-Grandfather Edgeworth's Victorian outlook, already quoted, is one of the rare exceptions—and yet Mrs. Wilson makes us very conscious of the process of social change. So delicate and subtle are the touches of observation that a hasty reader might miss them altogether. To make an exhaustive list of them would be tedious, but notice the references to Victorian melodramas on page 38, to the art of embroidery on page 41, to the chandeliers on page 42, to the feather bed and candle on page 55, to the family broughams and Book Meetings on page 59, to beards and Wesleyanism on page 73, to the proper attire in which to attend Shakespearean productions in Vancouver in the early years of this century on page 96, to the white calico nightdress on page 111, to the early architecture of Vancouver on pages 123 and 158. No detail of social life escapes Mrs. Wilson's attention: even the introduction of the flush toilet in Victorian England finds its way into the novel when Topaz triumphantly announces its woosh! woosh! to Matthew Arnold at the family dinner party with which the novel begins. We see the train replace the horse as a means of travel, and the automobile in turn replace the train; we see changing hair-styles, shifting fashions in dress, trends in interior decoration, changes in means of illumination, developments of dialect, slang and idiom, shifts in religious emphasis and observance. All of these things, together with the transmutations of little girls into aunts, great-aunts, and old women, combine to make *The Innocent Traveller* a fascinating journey through time.

IV   *The Journey Motif*

But the novel is also a fascinating journey through space, a sort of fictional travelogue. In the early chapters we get accurate and evocative descriptions of the English pottery towns, such as this:

> Elder House was set back by its "own grounds which surrounded it" from the Waterloo Road which, as the main thoroughfare from Bloxum to Ware, bore most of the traffic between the two manufacturing towns and their small grim satellites, and was, owing to its general undeniable drabness, a depressing street. Yet it was an exciting street, too. The Waterloo Road was exciting to Topaz and to Hannah because

it carried the daily life of the towns, and because it was important, and because of its multiplicity of small brick shops which contained people, sporadic genteel rows of brick houses which contained people, incroppings of residential brick splendour which contained magnates, brick public-houses radiating their own peculiar stale allure, posters advertising shockingly the dramas at the Bloxum Blood Tub, here a brick Chapel and there a brick Chapel, and, walking up and down the rather narrow pavements in front of all these bricks, the people of the towns with their own private stories. (p. 38)

In the middle section we are treated to a long, perceptive, and often poetic description of the varied landscapes of Canada from Quebec in the east to Vancouver in the west. Although Mrs. Wilson has always played down the role of conscious Canadianism in her work, it is difficult to see these loving descriptions as anything but her fervent tribute to her adopted country.

As the ladies come near to Canada on their Atlantic voyage, they see the glory of the Northern Lights:

That night the sky was lit from zenith to horizon by Northern Lights. Rachel and Topaz, niece and aunt, leaning at the ship's rail, saw a long and wavering luminous plume of pale-golden colour ascend in the north. The light fanned out and raced to the midmost topmost sky where a black whorl took shape and poured forth a cataract of glowing green. Successive cataracts of light issued from the whorl and became banners which flapped in silence across half the sky made vaster by the antics of the unexplained and ungovernable heavens. From the left of the spreading whorl, which changed shape and character as the onlookers gazed upon it, came a glow of dull crimson. The crimson ran rapidly down to meet the black ocean, changing and doubling and spreading as it ran. The colossal performance of the Northern Lights was exaggerated up up up, on and on, down down and across; and beyond and behind the zenith it encroached upon the southern sky. For time immeasurable and lost the heavens continued to ripple and wave with light, sometimes ghastly, always incomparable, filling the diminutive travellers beside the ship's railing with unprecedented awe. (p. 97)

And Topaz sees this spectacle as a happy portent that they have
made the right decision in coming to Canada. Similarly, Rachel,
as their train speeds through the jackpines north of Lake Su-
perior, feels the worry and fret drop away from her:

> Although Rachel would always be prone to anxiety, she had
> for ever, now, a fundamental peace—because she was where
> she liked to be. She was in essence as much a Canadian as
> those who had trodden Canada's wooded shores two hun-
> dred years before, or their descendants. (p. 113)

In the foothills of Alberta the normally unemotional Rachel has
a moment of mystical vision in response to the beauty of the
Canadian scene:

> In the gullies of the little hills through which they now
> passed there were aspens and birches whose leaves the early
> frost had turned from green to gold. The birches with their
> white maidenly stems and honey-yellow leaves shone against
> the dark conifers. Far to the north of them, but still east of
> the Rockies, east of Jasper House, the Athabasca River flowed
> widely through a land that was all gold. Golden golden
> golden shone the birch trees in the sunshine in that northern
> land from north to south, from east to west, spiked here and
> there by dark conifers. Few travellers along the brave steel
> way had ever heard of this golden world. But here, as the
> train hurried towards the mountains, Rachel looked up at
> the railway cutting and saw, for one moment, poised alone
> against the blue sky, a single slender white-stemmed aspen
> tree whose golden leaves trembled and shone and sang in
> the sunshine. It was there. It was gone. It was hers. (p. 119)

The Rockies fill Annie, characteristically, with a sense of religious
awe: "The Lord doeth wonderful things," she marvels. (p. 120)
    In the latter stages of the novel, Vancouver becomes a living
presence. Indeed there are premonitory references to it almost
from the very beginning of the novel:

> And the wind was blowing, too, among the great undis-
> covered pine trees in the yet unnamed place far away where
> some day Topaz Edgeworth would live and die. In this place
> Topaz would some day write and receive many letters, but no

one could yet send letters there. This place was still silent
and almost unknown. (pp. 36-37)

When they finally reach the city, it is first described panorami-
cally:

> If you arrive in Vancouver on a fine day and go up into a
> high place, to Little Mountain perhaps or even to the top of
> some high office building, you will come under the immediate
> spell of the mountains to the north of you, and of dark conif-
> erous forests. You will see high headlands sloping westwards
> into the Pacific Ocean, and islands beyond. And then you will
> turn again and look across the blue inlet at the mountains
> which in their turn look down upon the grace and strength
> of the Lions' Gate Bridge, upon the powerful flow of the
> Narrows, upon English Bay, upon the harbour, and upon
> the large city of Vancouver. (p. 123)

Gradually its details accumulate: its architecture, its history, its
sights and sounds, its social life. Its beauty becomes part of them:

> It was not long before the contours of the mountains became
> part of their lives. There was the Sleeping Beauty, lying
> nobly to the sky. There were the Lions rising sculptured,
> remote, indifferent. Smoke of fires trailed delicately through
> the trees. Along the topmost generous curve of the westward
> hills, pine trees cut sharply against the coloured evening
> skies, and there were always the sounds of the sirens of ships
> and the cries of the sea-gulls—sounds of ocean. (p. 125)

The novel ends in the streets of Vancouver, on the afternoon of
Topaz' funeral, as the sea-gulls fly overhead towards the vast
Pacific:

> The sea-gulls were flying westwards in their ordained eve-
> ning flight, in twos, threes, and companies, high overhead on
> account of the wind. . . . The customary westward flight of
> the sea-gulls over the sea, through the evening sky, was . . .
> a curious and ravishing sight. (p. 276)

V *Elegiac Elements*

That passage, obviously, has poetic and symbolic overtones, and thus serves as a convenient bridge to our consideration of *The Innocent Traveller* as an elegiac poem. There is a sense in which this novel has affiliations as close with Donne's "Anniversaries" and Milton's "Lycidas" as with the novels of Jane Austen and Arnold Bennett. Like the "Anniversaries" and "Lycidas," *The Innocent Traveller* laments and offers consolation for the death of a beloved individual; like them it sets this individual death in the context of the universal problem of Time and Eternity; like them it is a closely woven fabric of recurrent images and symbols.

It is as an elegiac poem that *The Innocent Traveller* is most clearly and intricately a consummate work of art. It is consciously but never self-consciously built and bulwarked. It begins with the epigraph from Donne already quoted which establishes the melancholy motif of life as the drop of water in a moving stream; it ends with this passage from Donne's *Devotions* which offers consolation in the awareness of the triumphant soul escaped from the dust of the flesh:

> The Bell rings out; the pulse thereof is changed; the tolling was a faint and intermitting pulse, upon one side; this stronger, and argues more and better life. His soule is gone out. . . . His soule is gone; whither? Who saw it come in, or who saw it goe out? No body; yet every body is sure, he had one, and hath none. . . . This soule, this Bell tells me, is gone out; Whither? Who shall tell mee that? . . . mine owne Charity; I aske that; and that tels me, He is gone to ever-lasting rest, and joy and glory.
> . . . We are . . . transported, our dust blowne away with prophane dust, with every wind. (pp. 276-77)

The first scene of the novel sets before us a cosy, comfortable, prosperous family dinner party; the last scene is of the youngest's funeral and the seagulls heading out at evening across the wastes of the Pacific. All the way through the novel images and symbols recur which alternately mourn and console, terrify and solace us.

Topaz is as "innocent as a poached egg," but underneath all life is an ultimate chasm:

> If Father had ever faltered in his faith, how deep would have been the crack, the fissure, the ultimate chasm into which he would have fallen. You and I, who pick our way unsurely amongst the appalling wreckage of our time, patching the crack here, avoiding the split there, anticipating the unsure footing, rejoicing in a bit of solid ground, and going ahead until we again trip and fall on our noses—we can take our troubles much more easily than Father could have done. (pp. 9-10)

Time is but a "strangely moving curtain" (p. 16) behind which members of the family mysteriously disappear. Upon this moving curtain, some few inscribe sweeping curves, but ordinary persons such as Topaz make merely temporary dots of colour:

> The day is over. The earth turns, and seven times turning brings Friday again. The weeks hasten by. Where are the weeks? They are lost in the years. Aunty's long life inscribes no sweeping curves upon the moving curtain of Time. She inscribes no significant design. Just small bright dots of colour, sparkling dots of life. (p. 243)

Even the most violent exertions cannot fundamentally alter Time's curtain, or halt its inexorable movement forward. The designs have been blocked out in advance, and we must accept them, however terrible they may be:

> There came a day when those who strained their eyes and looked forwards could see the forms of designs blocked out upon the future. These designs took shape and meaning with the present and with the past. Men did not need to be prophets to discern these patterns. Bombs would explode, men would drown, cities would burn, peoples would flee, dissension and faith would prevail, the pattern of suffering was clear. The future ceased to be a peaceful obscurity blocked by a concrete tomorrow which could be reached out to and almost touched as the planet revolved. The future (which was really one with the present and the past) became shockingly discernible. And beyond visibility it was

to a point implicit and to be believed. As the planet re-
volved making day and night against the patterned curtain
of Time, men painted daily in violent colours of noise and
flame and with an infinite unexpected detail of private living
the terrible designs upon the curtain. With the revolving of
the planet the painted many-dimensioned curtain slipped
slowly by and joined the past while men busied themselves
painfully about the present and the future. Or it seemed that
as the curtain on which men were painting, with extreme
difficulty, slipped backwards, men proceeded forwards
against the curtain at a snail's pace into a future already in
being. The voice speaking from the field of battle had always, in the nature of things, been prepared to speak. The
battle had always been, and was completed before it had
begun. (pp. 257-58)

But against this inevitability of horror we can set moments of
vision, glimpses of beauty, "the permanence of the impermanent":

While these events were disclosed in the world of Time,
there was a timeless and impersonal world to which men
turned and in which they found momentary refreshment.
The permanence of the fleeting and prodigal joy of this timeless world was without responsibility or question. The un-
earthly light of morning on the flank of the hill departs and
is eternal and no one can prevail against it. The permanence of the impermanent frail flower is for ever. So is the
sunshine on clover and the humming bees. The teasing whis-
per of the little wave on the shingle turns and always creeps
in again. The beauty of structure of a tree or of a mountain
changes but will never change. In these satisfying things
men refreshed themselves painfully yet with delight. (p. 258)

And so the characters like Topaz who stand for "the permanence of the impermanent," who may be mere evanescent drops of
water but who sparkle for their moment in the sun, are compared to birds, trees, flowers—things brief but beautiful. Topaz
is a fly, (p. 23) a twittering bird, (p. 44) a thrush, (p. 60) "a
milder Maenad with satin white skin, dancing heavily and happily, excited before the flickering shrine, carefree among the
olive trees, calling to the other boys and girls," (p. 89) a water-

glider "running about on the top of pleasant weed-fringed pools,"
(p. 103) "the dimpling of the water caused by the wind," (p. 105)
"a poor volatile bird," (p. 275) "a memory, a gossamer." (p. 275)

As this list suggests, imagery and symbolism of water and of
birds predominate. Water appears in the Donne epigraph, as the
drop in the stream; it reappears when Topaz' early life is compared to a canal "soundly constructed by her progenitors" and
"well administered by those now in passing":

> The banks of this smooth canal were pleasant, and pre-
> sented much variety to her, not in scenery, but in people
> who were seen in passing—to whom Topaz eagerly spoke,
> nodded, or waved when possible, whatever their station or
> occupation—and objects, which she pointed out with many
> lively comments. Except for a period when she passed
> through a long and dark tunnel, when, distraught, she did not
> know where to turn (but the way led straight on regardless
> of her despair), her journey was comfortable and well-condi-
> tioned. (p. 69)

Water recurs when Topaz is compared to a water-glider on a
summer pool:

> Unencumbered by boots or boats they run, seldom wetting
> their feet and, one supposes, unaware of the dreadful deeps
> below them, in which other beings more heavily weighted
> are plunged, and swim or sink, caught in the mud or en-
> tangled by the debris of circumstance and human relations;
> and sometimes these heavier beings encounter acute sorrow
> or acute joy or dull despair of which the water-gliders know
> nothing. Two or three times in her hundred years Aunty's foot
> slipped, below the surface of her pool, but only for a moment
> —albeit a long moment—and then she got caught in entangling
> sorrow and this caused her personal suffering. She at once,
> on recovery, resumed her running to and fro, and, quite
> unaware of the realities of the lives of the people whom she
> met day by day, she went eagerly laughing on. So, equipped
> as lightly as a water-glider of considerable education, she
> got on the train. (pp. 103-4)

That passage is followed immediately by another involving water
symbolism:

It was about half a century later that a great-grandson of the Grandmother's, walking home beside the Rideau Canal in Ottawa, stopped to light a cigarette and looked over the railing at the rather still water of the canal. There came a small invisible wind which ran rapidly along the surface of the water and made its presence known by the sudden pretty dimpling and wrinkling of the stream, and by the deflection of some dry leaves whose time had come to fall. The leaves were carried by the small vagrant wind down the slow-moving canal and sailed for a while until the sluggish current bore them to a cluster of waste twigs and lately fallen leaves at the canal's edge, and no one noticed them any more after that. The wind passed, and the water was again still, and the disturbance was forgotten. (p. 104)

It is not surprising that when Topaz has to read a poem to the ladies of the Minerva Club in Vancouver she chooses Matthew Arnold's "The Buried Life," where the image of life as a flowing stream appears once more:

"The eye sinks inward, and the heart lies plain,
And what we mean, we say, and what we would, we know.
A man becomes aware of his life's flow,
And hears its winding murmur; and he sees
The meadows where it glides, the sun, the breeze . . .
. . . And then he thinks he knows
The hills where his life rose,
And the sea where it goes." (p. 253)

Topaz comments, "My life rose in Staffordshire, and I suppose it's going out in the Pacific Ocean." (p. 253) Twenty pages later, we remember that prophecy, as on the afternoon of her funeral the sea-gulls seek the sea.

There is nothing novel about Ethel Wilson's use of water imagery: it is the traditional Platonic symbolism of the individual life as the drop of water which falls into the stream to find its way to the ocean of eternity and back to the sky and earth by evaporation and condensation in an endless cycle. But the effortless and subtle way in which it is used to knit together the phases of her story is admirably managed.

As for the imagery and symbolism of birds, we have already

seen how Topaz is compared at intervals throughout the novel
to a bird. Sometimes other characters are compared to birds:
when the ladies get into the Canadian train, we are told that "they
settled, crying and exclaiming, like shore birds" (p. 102); and
when, at a prairie railway station, the cry "All aboard!" comes,
"they turned and ran like chickens." (p. 118) But these early
examples are mere images; it is in the final pages of the novel
that birds take on symbolic status.

Sea-gulls dominate these final pages. The whole of Chapter
XXVI, "Sea-gulls in the City," is devoted to them, and they keep
recurring until they make their final appearance in the last line
before the epilogue from Donne. What do these gulls symbolize?
The gulls are proud, majestic, indifferent, wild, and cruel:

> The big white sea-gull has no heart of love. He is beautiful,
> strong, calculating, and rapacious. He does not love his own
> kind or human kind. He barely tolerates them. This carnal
> and lawless bird is slave to nothing but his own insatiable
> appetite. (pp. 260-61)

They represent something primitive and ferocious:

> Vancouver runs down to the sea. This way it runs down to
> the salt inlet. That way it runs down to the salt creek. East
> to west it runs to the Pacific Ocean. The hungry arrogant
> sea-gulls possess the water-front. Ships come into the har-
> bour from up the coast, from down the coast, from across the
> gulf, and again from the Orient, too, they come. The arro-
> gant greedy birds escort the ships to harbour, screaming
> and wheeling about the stern. Sometimes the sea-gulls fly
> over the city streets, and their mewing cries disturb the busy
> or abstracted minds of townspeople going about their busi-
> ness. Something shakes for an instant the calm of a man
> crossing the street when he hears the cry of a gull above the
> traffic, something that is not a sound but a disturbing, for-
> gotten, unnamed desire, a memory. Java, Dubrovnik, the
> Hebrides. What is it? (p. 261)

One gull stares through the window at Topaz, now a frail old
lady:

> One gull, however, really settles on the window-ledge. He

bows and bows, and presses himself against the pane, staring at the Great-Aunt in his avaricious way. He is not interested that she talks and laughs to him. He is completely
interested in food. There is no more food. At last the sea-gull
accepts and despises this fact, so he flies away. He looks grey
from beneath, but the breaking sunlight from above outlines
his strong wings in bright transient silver. (pp. 262-63)

If we had not guessed before, we know from that passage that
the gulls are the symbols of Death. And we are therefore quite
prepared for their reappearance on the afternoon of Topaz's funeral.

VI *Thematic Patterns*

The Innocent Traveller is in some sense an elegiac poem; it is
also a parable of the human condition. Together, the members
of the Edgeworth family constitute a microcosm of humanity, and
their life stories a microcosm of human history. Conventional and
patriarchal like Father, saintly and reverential like Annie, anxiously dutiful and practical like Rachel, gay, innocent and irresponsible like Topaz, earth-bound, pleasure-loving but sensible like
Rose, cunning and inconsistent like Yow—all men and women play
out their assigned roles against the curtain of Time, and then disappear into Eternity. Each has his momentary pleasures—Father
his sense of order, Annie her moments of religious communion,
Rachel her glimpses of peace and beauty, Topaz her constant
chattering enthusiasm, Rose her books and her tennis, Yow his
gambling evenings—and then departs. Each tries to establish
some relationship with the eternal, the permanent, the divine—
Father through Wesleyanism and bourgeois values, Annie through
the evangelical churches, Rachel through nature's beauty, Topaz
through her three loyalties to Queen, Gladstone, and Father, Rose
through literature and sport, Yow through the continuity of his
family—but each must release his grip when "Elusive, unheard,
some significant moment of Time has just struck. She must go
home." (p. 243) Some, like Father, are blithely unaware of the
chasm beneath them, others, like Rachel, are perpetually anxious,
still others, like Topaz, glide gaily on the surface of the stream—
but all eventually sink from sight.

What, then, is the consolation? Has Mrs. Wilson any affirmation to offer us? Not, I think, a conventionally religious affirmation: the frequent references to organized religion throughout the book are all tinged with irony, and the suggestion is that all religions are equally good—and equally imperfect. That there is a God whom all men imperfectly worship is certainly suggested, but with the possible exception of Annie none of the characters gets much permanent satisfaction from his religious aspirations. It is Topaz rather than Annie who dominates the book, and in her there is a large infusion of paganism, of the Greek spirit of epicureanism. If there is an underlying philosophy of life in the novel, it is a kind of hedonistic humanism, expressed most fully in Topaz' "gay purity" or innocent gaiety.

Nature is beautiful—but it has no sympathy with human aspirations. The heavens are "unexplained and ungovernable." (p. 97) The Northern Lights seem to say "I can do this again any minute that I want to. I can do more than this. I am independent of you, uncontrolled by you, indifferent to you, and you know nothing at all about Me." (p. 99) Indeed nature, for all its momentary beauty, is fundamentally hostile to man:

> And far to the north, and to the south too, unnumbered, uncountable, stood the crowded jackpines, and among them lay dark, unreachable, anonymous lakes of blank water. And soon all this country and north to Hudson's Bay and beyond would be sealed with iron cold, and with silence broken only by the ultimate shot-like crack of frozen wood or water. And the train ran on and on, and the jackpines showed no sign that they would ever come to an end. (p. 114)

> All day the illimitable prairie spread before them and slipped behind them. Far to the north (and to the south) the prairie spread, defeating imagination, like eternity. They did not know that further north still were great irregular lakes, and rivers, and a great river flowing to the Arctic Ocean, where only a few of the hardiest white men had been. They could not tell, speeding comfortably across the yellow stubble of the prairie, that winter would come and seal, and petrify, and drive away birds, and exact a difficult life and death from fur-bearing animals and their hunters, and maintain in

rigidity and without mercy a whole empire in the north.
(p. 118)

And yet it is from this fundamentally hostile nature that men
snatch glimpses of beauty, "the beauty of structure of a tree or
of a mountain" which "changes but will never change," (p. 258)
and find delight in "the permanence of the impermanent frail
flower." (p. 258) And in the face of nature's hostility—so hostile
on the prairies that it drives women mad (p. 117)—they manage
to build a civilization:

> But as they looked abroad on the bare prairie and over little
> groups of small angular buildings, she could see nothing
> to confirm the queerly Latin name in this so very new prairie
> town. But then Aunty could not look forward and see a
> vigorous city of brick and stone and wood, of industries,
> of grain elevators, and a seat of government, with a man-
> made lake, and hand-planted parks, and a thriving centre
> of a far-flung community of prosperous wheat farmers. She
> could not see the courage and vision that absurdly dared to
> call this place Regina. (p. 116)

Thus *The Innocent Traveller* is, in its quiet unemphatic way, a
testament to the tenacity, gaiety and courage of the human spirit.

VII   *Style, Structure, and Tone*

Something about the style and structure of the novel remains
to be said. Its most remarkable technical achievement is its management of time, perhaps the most difficult of all the problems
which face the novelist. Mrs. Wilson suggests that all Time is
perpetually present and yet perpetually flowing, and she conveys
this double sense by the use of premonition and memory, flash-
forward and flash-back, and by the patient skill with which she
notes all the tiny changes in the appearance, status, dress, speech
habits, gestures, and relationships of her characters. To give
the sense of a hundred years passing in a novel of less than three
hundred pages is no mean feat, but it is one which Mrs. Wilson
accomplishes.

A second facet of her technical skill is her adroit handling of
the point of view. The point of view keeps shifting—from Topaz

to Father to Annie to Rachel to Yow to Rose and back again—
and yet we are never awkwardly aware of the shift, or conscious
of any disunity. It is like the shifting of gears in a finely engineered
automatic transmission: it is done so silently and smoothly that
we never notice it.

Structurally, the novel is a triumph, with part balancing part
and each part interlocking with its neighbours. We go from
Donne in the epigraph to Donne in the Epilogue; from Matthew
Arnold the dinner guest in Chapter I to Matthew Arnold the
author of "The Buried Life" in Chapter XXV; from Topaz as
"me, the youngest" on page 16 to Topaz as "me the youngest"
on page 275; from the drop of water to the stream to the canal
to the pool to the rivers to the ocean; from Topaz the twittering
bird on page 44 to Topaz the poor volatile bird trying to escape
its cage of flesh on page 275. The novel is a continuous fabric of
interwoven motifs.

Each successive chapter is a unit in itself—so much so that
several of them were published independently as periodical
sketches prior to book publication—and yet each chapter grows
out of the one which preceded it and blends into the one that
follows it. Such chapters as "I Have a Father in the Promised
Land," which was published in the *New Statesman and Nation,*
or "The Innumerable Laughter," which was published in *Orion IV,*
or "Nuts and Figs," which would have found a ready welcome
with the editor of any magazine—such chapters can be read and
appreciated as self-contained short stories, and yet in the context of the novel their significance is greatly enriched.

Finally the humour of the novel, mention of which is long over-
due. Humour, of almost every variety from broad farce to subtle
irony, is a constant element in the novel. The very first chapter
is brilliantly funny, presenting us as it does with the spectacle of
little Topaz telling the austere Matthew Arnold of the delights
of the Edgeworth's new flush toilet, or climbing under the dinner
table to examine the assembled family's shoes, legs and nether-
garments. "Nuts and Figs," retailing Great-Grandfather's double
proposal at the age of ninety, is hilarious from beginning to end,
while "I Have a Father in the Promised Land" subtly combines
pathos and farce. Topaz' English bicycle, which is so obstreperous
a machine that she takes to wheeling it with her rather than
riding upon it, is another rich source of humour. Perhaps the

funniest scene of all is that late one, Chapter XXVII, "Unlike the
Saintly Elijah," in which the ancient Aunt Topaz makes her last
sally from her apartment, on a very hot day, in search of ice-
cream:

"Oh, Miss Edgeworth," Miss Umplethwaite says anxiously,
"told you you shouldn't have come, I said——"

"Don't begin saying 'I told you so,'" says Aunty with
asperity. "I can't bear being rushed along in the heat. You're
rushing me. Me legs don't seem to be functioning. There's
something wrong with me legs."

"Oh, Miss Edgeworth," says the alarmed companion (the
very first time out!), "lean on me, I'll help you along. I'll put
my arm round you!" And so they walk, sweltering, each
clutching the other.

"It's paralysis," says Aunty, irritated. "Never before in my
family. I can't make it out. I can't feel me legs. I can't use
them. OH! Elijah Jones was paralysed, he was a very saintly
man was Elijah, handsome too; there were three Elijah
Joneses in wheel-chairs, two of them with water on the knee
and one paralysed, in three generations. That's why they
stopped using the name Elijah in the Jones family. Oh, this
is terrible. I can't even use me feet! Miss Umple, Miss Umple!
I'm going to fall!"

Miss Umplethwaite is distracted. She seizes Aunt Topaz
more firmly. She glances down. Wreathed around Aunty's
feet are her good white calico drawers. Descending they
had impeded her. Descended, they wrap her feet around.
She is helpless to move.

"Lift up a foot, Miss Edgeworth, lift up a foot," implores
Miss Umplethwaite, hotter than ever. Passers-by rouse from
their lethargy and take interest. People turn and smile kindly
enough.

"I can't lift a foot. I'm paralysed! I've had a stroke, I do
declare!" says Aunty, shocked.

"Oh, yes, you can, Miss Edgeworth. Try. Try. It's only
your . . . ," murmurs Miss Umplethwaite, wrestling. She bends
down and lifts up one of Aunt Topaz' strangely large and
heavy feet, and wriggles the garment off; she lifts up the
other foot; and wriggles the other part of the garment off;

she whips the calico drawers up into a bundle, tucks them under her arm, and faces the world with a flush.

Great-Aunt Topaz is amazed. "Eh, it's me knickers!" she says astonished. She kicks out with one leg, kicks out with the other, and finds them free and active. Distress fades to surprise, to pleasure on her face. She steps out nimbly. She is pleased. (pp. 269–70)

CHAPTER 5

The Equations of Love (1952)

I *Introduction*

THE *Equations of Love* contains two short novels, or novellas, *Tuesday and Wednesday* and *Lilly's Story*. (*Lilly's Story* was published separately under that title in the United States.) In some ways, the two novellas are quite different, and scarcely seem to belong in a single volume. *Tuesday and Wednesday* deals with a fairly large cast of sleazy lower class inhabitants of Vancouver, whereas *Lilly's Story* concentrates almost entirely on the single character of its title, and most of its action occurs in the country and a Fraser Valley village. The action of *Tuesday and Wednesday*, as its title suggests, is restricted to two days, whereas *Lilly's Story* extends over some thirty or forty years. *Tuesday and Wednesday* derives its interest almost entirely from the subtle interplay of relationships between a group of characters, but *Lilly's Story* has as its central character a woman who cares little for human relationships, other than that of mother and child, and who single-mindedly pursues social respectability and financial security for herself and her daughter. And whereas all the characters in *Tuesday and Wednesday* are victims—of death, loneliness, frustration, poverty, and dinginess—Lilly is quite clearly a victor. The *Tuesday and Wednesday* characters are lazy, inert, shiftless, irresponsible and weak-willed; Lilly is industrious, determined, thrifty, deeply responsible when the interests of her daughter are concerned, and the very embodiment of the will that triumphs over adverse circumstances. The first novella is set almost entirely indoors, in shabby, dingy rooms, or in grey, mean city streets drenched in rain or shrouded in mist; the second is set preponderantly in the outdoors, amidst natural scenery that is invigorating, beautiful, and multicoloured.

Both novels employ many images drawn from animate nature, but the animals and birds in *Tuesday and Wednesday* are mainly tame, domestic, and friendly whereas those in *Lilly's Story* are wild and hostile, birds and beasts of prey.

The similarities between the two novellas, however, are suggested by the book's title, and by the epigraph from *Bleak House* which the stories share:

> "Now, my young friends," [said Mr. Chadband] "what is this Terewth . . . firstly (in a spirit of love) what is the common sort of Terewth . . ."

An equation may be any of three things: mathematically, it is a statement expressing the equality of two quantities; chemically, it is the symbolic representation of a reaction, stating first the substances which react and secondly the products of their reaction; logically, it means the tendency to error in observation and reasoning resulting from individual bias. I am not sure in which of these three senses Mrs. Wilson used the term in her title, but I suggest that she may have had all three meanings in mind. First of all, I think she is implying that love takes many forms, and that these two stories exhibit its variety, the many equations by which it may be expressed. In *Tuesday and Wednesday* there is the married love between Mort and Myrt, which is a mixture of habit, companionship, sensuality, and shared frustration; the love between Mort and Eddie, which is basically comradeship but grows to something very like the greatest kind of love when Mort loses his life attempting to save his friend's; the love of Victoria May for Myrtle, which begins as a search for companionship but ends as compassion; Myrtle's love for Victoria May, which is the kind of tepid tenderness one extends to a lonely relative; Mrs. Emblem's love for her three husbands, which was a mixture of sensuality, possessiveness, and a desire to give comfort; and Mrs. Emblem's love for Myrtle, after Mort's death, which is sheer animal comfort, the pressure of flesh on flesh. In *Lilly's Story*, the emphasis is on Lilly's love for her daughter Eleanor, which is a kind of blind maternal instinct, but there is also Yow's love for Lilly, which is lust touched with cruelty, Yow's love for Mrs. Hastings, which is pure and dutiful, the love of servant for mistress, Mr. Meakins' love for Lilly, which is sentimental and evanescent, the love between Lilly and the hospital matron, which is mutual respect and affection, Lilly's love for Paddy Wilkes, a brief but tumultous passion, Mr. Sprockett's love for his wife, which we are told was "not rapture . . . but perfect satisfaction," (p. 257) and the love between Mr. Sprockett and Lilly, which is a desire for comfort and companionship between two elderly, lonely people.

The plots of the two novellas are also equations of love in the chemical sense: we see characters and circumstances interact in love, and watch the resultant products. Mort's love for Eddie, for example, sets up a kind of chain reaction: it leads to his own transfiguration, when in vainly attempting to save his friend's life he grows from an inert victim into a tragic hero; his death, in turn, leads to the transfiguration of Victoria May, who from being a mousy nobody suddenly becomes a self-forgetful but self-confident celebrator of the hero, to the maturing of Myrtle into a woman confident and self-possessed, and to the transformation of Mrs. Emblem from an easy-going, self-indulgent sensualist into a kind of eternal mother-figure, serenely watching over her troubled "children." A similar but singly focussed reaction occurs in *Lilly's Story*: as a result of her series of love relationships with Yow, Ranny Griffiths, Eleanor, the Butlers, the matron, Mr. Meakins, Paddy, and Mr. Sprockett, Lilly is transformed from a silly, shiftless, irresponsible girl into a sensible, self-reliant, and eminently responsible and respectable woman.

But that the third, personal, sense of equation is also present is implied by the epigraph from *Bleak House*, which suggests that we are all biased and that it is difficult if not impossible to answer Pilate's question, "What is truth?" Both novellas demonstrate the ambiguity of all moral judgments. To the police, Mort's death was mere drunken sloppiness; to Myrt, it was first a deliberate insult and injury, and later the act of a hero; to Victoria May it was a triumphant and splendid act of self-sacrificial love. Similarly, Lilly might be described as a slut, a liar, and a thief; but from another point of view she seems chaste, truthful, and honest.

There are other bonds which link *Tuesday and Wednesday* and *Lilly's Story*. Both lay much stress on loneliness, fear, and alienation; both, on the other hand, have much to say also about companionship, innocence, and a sense of belonging. Both present us with characters who are superficially unattractive, but almost all of whom eventually win our respect or at least our pity. Both show us handicapped characters in conflict with adverse circumstances, but managing to snatch from these adversities a humble but by no means despicable triumph. Both, in short, give us glimpses of the boredom, the horror, and the occasional glory of ordinary human life.

II *Tuesday and Wednesday*

One aspect of Ethel Wilson's skill as a narrator is her ability to arouse our interest in and compassion for the most apparently unsympathetic of characters. Nowhere is this capacity more evident than in *Tuesday and Wednesday*. One feels in reading this novella that Mrs. Wilson has deliberately chosen the most drab, sleazy, lazy and generally unpromising cast she could imagine, and has set herself the task of eliciting our sense of fellow-feeling for its members. She has put this cast into the most drab and dreary of streets and rooms, immersed their environment in turn in the most dreary of weather (there is mist, drizzle or rain on almost every page of the second half), and assigned them roles in a plot which consists of the most mundane of business and social arrangements culminating in an unnecessary and graceless death. The miracle is that in spite of all this, the novella grips and holds our attention and provokes in us, at least to a degree, the emotions which we associate with high tragedy.

A. *Characterization: Mort*

The "hero" of *Tuesday and Wednesday* is Mortimer Johnson, a shiftless gardener and handyman, the empty boredom of whose life is established in the sentences which introduce him to us:

> Because Mortimer Johnson's bedroom faced westwards and was darkened as much as possible, the sun had risen fairly high before Mort woke up. Then, because he had to get up some time or other, he got up.[1]

But immediately afterwards Mrs. Wilson begins the process of eliciting fellow-feeling for this unpromising character. Although Mort is lazy and self-indulgent, he has compassion for his wife:

> He got up quickly and gently pulled the grey blankets back
> again over the warm bed because he did not want to disturb
> his wife Myrtle who still slept. Mort emerged from bed in
> his underclothes and stood sleepily regarding the curved pile
> in the bed, which was Myrtle. (p. 3)

But exactly what are his feelings for his wife? The uncertainty,
the variability of human responses is one of the dominant themes
of this book. That Mort's feeling for his wife is not merely self-
forgetful compassion but has undertones of self-regarding sensuality is suggested by the sentences which follow:

> He stretched and rubbed himself slowly over his stomach
> and sides and back and shoulders and arms. The feeling of
> the woollen combinations rubbing on his skin gave him a
> slow obscure pleasure. (p. 3)

Shortly afterwards we learn that there is more than a mixture of
compassion and sensuality involved in Mort's relations with his
wife: there are fear and anger as well. But out of this mixture of
responses emerges the simple human act of bringing his wife tea
in bed:

> After Mortimer had looked at his wife as he continued to
> rub himself, his early morning thought arose, the first thought
> of each morning. Was Myrtle pleased last night and will she
> be pleased this morning when she wakes up, or am I in
> wrong again, because if she acts like she did yesterday, I'll
> slug her. He then applied the usual solution of this important
> little puzzle and walked barefooted and picking up dust into
> the adjoining room which was kitchen and everything else,
> and struck a match and lighted the gas ring and put on the
> kettle for a cup of tea. When he had made the tea he put
> the things on a little tray the way Myrtle had taught him
> to do fifteen years ago, and then he brought the tray to
> the bedside and put it on the floor because everything else
> had something on it, and pulled up the blinds and let the
> morning in, but no air, and bent over Myrtle and poked
> her. (p. 5)

This sense of Mortimer as a curious mixture of selfishness and
selflessness, of irascibility and tenderness, is confirmed by every

other scene in which he appears. He is despicable and yet admirable. After breakfast he goes off to a new job—looking after the garden of Mrs. H. Y. Dunkerley—and for a little while he is the ideal working man:

> Mort was feeling contented and happy as he usually did at the beginning of a new job. He was efficient and experienced; he was a gardener, moreover, Myrtle had been in good humour; he was a good husband, the best of husbands, he had given her morning tea; Mrs. Dunkerley looked a nice little thing and he knew how to manage her. (p. 13)

But almost at once he begins to surround his morning innocence with falsehood. To win Mrs. Dunkerley's sympathy, he tells her that his wife Myrtle is sick. She is impressed, and brings him a cold beer; but when her husband unexpectedly arrives she deserts Mort at once, injures his vanity, and arouses his anger. We witness one of the many transfiguration scenes which punctuate this novel and underline its theme of human variability:

> The only person who was not feeling pleased was Mort. While not dangerous to women, he had a way with him and was vain. He had just been experiencing the pleasant sensation of his male power working nicely and smoothly on a pretty little woman—the wife of a lumber magnate, at that— when the pretty little woman had dropped him flat and had disappeared into the house without even looking back. This nice woman had not even introduced him to her husband— a backward jerking finger had sufficed—and the husband had not seen fit to honour him at all, even with a nod. He was, of course, unreasonable, but there you are. He felt reduced in size. His sense of injury mounted, and as Mrs. Dunkerley continued on the front verandah to ply her husband with two drinks, and then with food, and hang upon his lips, and forgot to tell that dumb Chink to give him some lunch, Mort's world changed. His angel, shuffling uneasily, was aware of this, and helplessly saw the turnover of Mort from successful male, successful gardener, old and trusted employee, unique landscaper, the husband possessed of an ailing but doting wife, to a working man insulted and snubbed by a rich man who no doubt had made his money

by graft, and the possessor of a wife who had to toil all day
on account of people like Mrs. Dunkerley. He had been
fawned upon, snubbed and forgotten by a rich woman for
what digging she could get out of him. See what Myrt would
say to this, and him slaving away in the heat! At this moment
the Chinese cook came out and nonchalantly said "Lunch"
and disappeared. Worse insult than any, to be ordered about
by a Chink. Mort strode to a sheltered spot to eat his lunch.
If this was the kind of place it was he wouldn't stay. (pp.
16–17)

On his way back to Vancouver proper from Mrs. Dunkerley's
estate, Mort undergoes another change of heart. He repents of
having wished an imaginary illness upon his wife and determines
to make it up to her:

> Mort stood and waited for the bus. He began to realize that
> without intending to, and simply because he had been late
> that morning, he had wished some kind of an illness on to
> Myrtle, which was too bad. He felt a warm protective feeling
> for her rising within him and wanted to do some little thing
> to make up for the disease which he had wished upon her.
> And so it happened . . . that he got off the bus and instead
> of going home he went to Eaton's Store. He thought he would
> get Myrtle a pair of nylons. . . . (p. 30)

In the store, boyishly eager over his anticipated purchase, he
encounters Mr. Dunkerley, who is buying stockings for *his* wife,
and again Mort is transfigured. Dunkerly is haughty and hostile,
and this "had a dampening effect on the little boy who was
Mort. In fact the little boy disappeared as through a trap-door,
and a slightly truculent man took his place." (p. 33)

This chance encounter—and there is much emphasis in the
novel on the part played by chance in human iife—leads Mort to
take refuge in a beer-parlour. There he meets his old friend
Pork, an undertaker's assistant, and after a few beers the two
friends go off to the funeral parlour where Pork works. This gives
Mrs. Wilson an opportunity to reveal Mort's character from a
very unusual angle of vision: his response to various types of
coffins. This revelation of character from an unusual angle is one
of the most conspicuous features of Mrs. Wilson's technique: we

may recall the under-the-dining-room-table view in *The Innocent Traveller,* and later in *Tuesday and Wednesday* we learn much about the characters of Mrs. Emblem and Victoria May Tritt from their respective manners of reading the newspaper. The strange mixture of boyish innocence, adolescent sentimentality, and adult responsibility which make up Mort's character are well evoked as he looks at the coffins:

> He was divided between a forbidding box covered with elephant grey and lined with off-white, and a fine job covered with purple brocaded velours and lined with heliotrope satin. Either of these coffins was suited to a certain aspect of Mort's temperament, but he preferred the richness of the purple. There'd be some satisfaction in being buried in something like that. If he wasn't afraid of Pork coming back he'd get in, just for the feel, but he knew Pork wouldn't like that. He now thought of Myrtle. He would choose one for her. After some difficulty and much sticking out of his lower lip and pinching his chin, he chose a coffin prettily lined with shining blue, and stood over it, looking down. He became sentimental, and then he became unhappy. He became luxuriously unhappy, and mysteriously elevated. He looked down into the soft blue satin and—plain as day—he saw Myrt lying there. This, then, was really the end of everything. This was what we come to; and then—no more; this— and no other. He saw Myrt's thin occasionally pretty face with its well-known look, the eyelids closed; and the circumstances of Myrt's death and funeral rose and encompassed him. Easy tears filled his eyes and he dried them with the back of his hand. He thought I haven't always been so good to Myrt as I ought to been, though God knows she'd drive you mad the way she acts sometimes but I bet I'll be sawry sometime for the things I done. (pp. 41–42)

Incidentally, the almost certainly symbolic use of colour in this passage is repeated at other points in the novella, but the whole question of colour symbolism will be treated below.

When Mort gets home, late, from the funeral parlour, he and his wife Myrtle have a quarrel, but the antics of a stray kitten relieve the tension and they go to bed as lovers. This, in short, is another transfiguration scene, and it is brought about through the agency of a kitten which is, here as elsewhere in the novel, a symbol of innocence. "The kitten," we read, "was irresistible in its bland innocence." (p. 62)

The manner of Mort's death is as ambiguous and variable as his life. On the second day of the novel, the Wednesday, he goes to seek a new job at a large market-garden, and dreams of a future in which he and Myrtle will live in idyllic innocence in a shack on that estate. Returning to Vancouver in the evening, he meets his old logger friend Eddie Hansen, who is very drunk and drags Mort down to the docks in search of his lost suitcase. There in the darkness Eddie falls into the water. Mort either falls or jumps in after him, and both men are drowned. Opinions of the nature of Mort's death vary all the way from the police view that, like Eddie, he was drunk (which he certainly was not) to Victoria May Tritt's view that he heroically dove in in an attempt to save his friend's life (which is not true either). The real truth is a confusion of motives and accidents, of fear and friendship, of cowardice and heroism.

B. *Characterization: Myrtle*

The ambiguity of Mort's character is paralleled by that of his wife, Myrt. She too is lazy—her apartment is always in a mess—sensual, selfish, inconsistent and unpredictable. Like Mort, she is given to sudden transfigurations, though in her case they are more deliberate: "She was a complete mistress (or victim) of the volte-face, of the turn-about, and this dubious possession was one of the reasons for her control and enslavement of Mort." (p. 6) Like Mort, too, who is a drunkard to the police and a hero to Victoria May Tritt, Myrtle appears very differently to different people. To Mort, in a beerily sentimental mood, she is "the finest little woman God ever made; everybody liked her and she was the refined type" (p. 37); but to the amiable Mrs. Emblem "Myrtle always acted kinda mean even when she was a kid." (p. 48) Her outstanding characteristic is her lazy self-indulgence, her conceited self-love. Her heavy eyelids, we are told, "were but the outward and physical sign of an inward and spiritual conceit." (p. 8) "Of all people, Myrtle loved herself in whatever guise she saw herself." (p. 8) Her favourite guise is that of the victim, the martyr, and her favourite mood is that of self-pity. She frequently assumes "the character of a woman universally put upon." (p. 10) She therefore quite welcomes the thought that in her widowhood she has been the victim of Mort's irresponsible drunkenness:

> And Vicky, who knew nothing of married love and married hate, of married joy and married fury, saw with a dawning understanding the dreadful thing about Myrtle Johnson— that she was content to have Morty die as she then thought he died; and that she did not much wish to believe what Vicky told her; and Vicky dimly apprehended that Myrtle in her self-love did not intend to cease being wronged by Morty in his death. (p. 122)

Vicky concludes that Myrtle is "a wicked wicked woman" (p. 122)—but even Myrtle, the least sympathetic character in the book, has some redeeming qualities. "She really loved him [Mort] in her own way." (p. 8) and we are told that if her parents had been alive she might have loved them, and that if she had had children she might have loved them too. She is kind to the most pathetic character of all, Victoria May Tritt, and when Victoria May has persuaded her that her husband died a hero's death Myrtle is able to remember him "with half grudging tenderness and with her best and sleazy love." (p. 128) Our final glimpse of her is of her loneliness (p. 128) and thus our final feeling for her is not irritation, nor contempt, but pity.

C. *Minor Characters*

About Mort and Myrt, the two central characters, are grouped a number of minor characters, and the two chief of these, Victoria May Tritt and Mrs. Emblem, make excellent foils for one another. Victoria May is mousy and shy; Mrs. Emblem is flamboyant and gregarious. Vicky is compared to "some poor dawg that nobody wants" (p. 25); Mrs. Emblem is "the jewel in the dark ear of the Ethiope." (p. 19)

Human loneliness is one of the main themes of *Tuesday and Wednesday*, and Victoria May Tritt is the very embodiment of loneliness. She is the perpetual outsider, painfully conscious of "her own inadequacy, her lack of small talk, her feeling of being the extra one wherever she was." (p. 25) She lives in "a timorous

world" (p. 25) and has to nerve herself up to visiting even her
cousin Myrtle. She is "the youngest Tritt girl, nothing more,
conveniently anonymous" (p. 64); "she is anonymous, as a fly
is anonymous." (p. 66) Her loneliness is at times insupportable:

> She is sufficient unto herself, in a parched way, and yet she
> is sometimes lonely with a vast loneliness that for a dreadful
> moment appals. She goes her way by day and by night and
> all is well enough; and then suddenly she is aware of a
> loneliness which is insupportable. What makes her suddenly
> aware and alone? It is not the crowd in the street, for the
> anonymity of the continually passing crowd suits her; it is,
> perhaps, the greeting with delight of woman with woman,
> of man with woman—not of man with man, which stirs
> nothing; it is the ascending again of the stairs and going into
> her bedroom and feeling in the dark for the light which
> hangs small and naked in the middle of the room; it is the
> emptiness of time and occupation, the desert that lies be-
> tween now and sleep; it is the inexplicable fusion of some-
> thing within her and something without. Yet she does not
> desire company; like the fakir who has for so long held his
> arm unused that it is now atrophied, so Miss Tritt's power
> of friendship is vanished, gone. The fakir forgets his useless
> arm; Miss Tritt forgets, on the whole, that she is lonely. (p.
> 67)

She is forever afraid of being the one left over:

> How many thousand times the same fear had descended on
> Vicky that now had descended upon her—the old familiar
> fear that the girls were going to pick sides for games, and
> no one would pick her, and at the end she would be left
> over and one of the captains would say to the other captain
> "And *you*'ll have to take Victoria May Tritt," and she would
> have to be taken; the fear that came as she looked from
> girl to girl; the malaise that came at the end of school and
> at the end of Sunday school, when all the other girls ran
> off home together or walked together, heads bent together,
> in twos or threes, all talking at once and then saying to
> each other "You come over to my place," "No, you come
> over to my place"; the fear that made her cross the road

to avoid speaking to someone she knew; the same fear that came when her mother used to dress her in her good dress and make her go out to a party to which all three Tritt girls had been invited ("Oh *Motherr*, do we *haff* to ask the youngest Tritt girl, she's a lemon!"); that familiar fear of people and their ways which possessed her. (p. 75)

And yet for all her sense of alienation and inadequacy, Victoria May is capable of heroism and of compassion. Her transfiguration comes as the result of Mort's death. Seeing that Myrtle is enjoying the luxury of self-pity and is happy to accept the police version of Mort's death, and knowing that Mort was not drunk (she had seen him, perfectly sober, go off toward the dock with the drunken Eddie), Vicky tells a splendid lie to the effect that Mort heroically dove into the water. She is "transformed beyond herself by death . . . and by her own compassion." (p. 120) She convinces Myrtle of the truth of her tale, and then relapses into her timorous self. But she will never be quite the same again:

The once-felt blaze of heat that had so warmed Victoria May as she stood over her cousin Myrtle did not of course long retain its virtue; but in solitude—which was to say in most of Victoria May's waking and sleeping life—she was often to be sustained by the contemplation of that moment and of that scene which her memory came habitually to recall, to fondle, to admire, and to enhance. (p. 128)

There is no sense of alienation in Mrs. Emblem, Myrtle's ample and affable aunt. She alone can "make Myrtle feel foolish and inadequate any time she wants to." (p. 7) She comes "puffing luxuriously into the dingy room" and spreads "her plump white hand over her wide soft bosom." (p. 19) She glories in the flesh and its pleasures—she has been "honest wife and true mistress" (p. 50) to three men already, and is contemplating a fourth marriage—and is "like a beautiful old baby." (p. 56) Just to look at her cheers people up: "Then her face cleared and resumed its customary happy and ingenuous expression—an expression which softened and pleased the hearts of strange people even on streetcars." (p. 21) She is "a comely golden old comedy actress playing her part very well," (pp. 23–24) she has "a golden lazy smile," (p. 25) and to Mort she appears as a "radiant vision, temporary rainbow." (p. 45)

But just as the mainly unhappy Victoria May has her moments of triumph, so the mainly happy Mrs. Emblem has her moments of fear:

> From time to time she works because she likes the extra money, and because although she is Mrs. Emblem and therefore a happy woman, she sometimes feels a certain vacuity which is not filled by cleaning and polishing her room, shopping (which usually means walking through the shops with one of her friends), going to a show, and playing whist or bridge with Mr. Thorsteinsen, Mr. Jacobs, and Maybelle. She is hardly aware of the poignant communications of sky, of birds, of ocean, forest, and mountain, although she thinks Vancouver is a nice place. She does not see around or beyond the tangible male or female human form and its appearance and peculiar requirements. I think, in order to be perfectly happy, she still needs to look after someone. (pp. 50–51)

She "is not lonely—exactly," but her lack of a fourth husband is for her a kind of loneliness, a deprivation similar to but less acute than Victoria May's. Like Victoria May, also, she has her finest moment when Mort dies: she comforts Myrtle with her ample flesh:

> Mrs. Emblem with her arms around Myrtle and her face against Myrtle's face thought out of her own experience. It's bad anyway, but when a husband dies drunk I guess it takes everything that might be sad or kind right away and I don't know what to say to her; and so she continued to hold Myrtle in silence. (p. 124)

Our last glimpse of her is of her sitting in the rocking-chair after Myrtle has gone to bed:

> And at last Myrtle went to bed solitary yet sustained, and she at last slept, and Aunty Emblem settled herself in the rocking chair in her slip with her coat round her shoulders, and, rocking a little, soon slept. Mrs. Emblem and the kitten, who had much in common, woke from time to time, wandered about a little to see that all was well, settled again and slept. (p. 127)

Mrs. Emblem, then, like the kitten, is a symbol of innocence—innocence in that special sense in which Mrs. Wilson uses the word: as a direct, wide-eyed, unjaded, enthusiastic response to life.

D. *Place*

Mrs. Wilson, then, has made us realize the extraordinariness of the most ordinary characters, has revealed the element of the heroic in the timorous, of the unselfish in the self-indulgent. She has accomplished this for the most part indirectly, by concentrating upon the tiny, subtle, self-revealing gesture, expression, tone of voice, gait or attitude. A similar skill is evident in her handling of the environment of these characters. The environments express the characters, and the characters in turn express their environments: there is a constant interplay and mutual interdependence. Myrt's room and Mrs. Emblem's room are both perfectly ordinary rooms, such as are multiplied a million times across Canada, but each expresses, and is expressed by, its occupant. All of Myrt's shiftless, untidy, dingy self is in her bedroom:

> When Mort had gone, Myrtle sat up and really looked about her. What she saw was their bedroom and because she was so accustomed to these two rooms (with sink) at the top of the house off Powell Street, she did not see that the room was dingy and needed cleaning; that it was not carpeted except by one small bedside mat (which was the cause of daily and nightly outrage and something near madness to the two old men living below); that the bureau was littered with brush, pins, comb, Eno's, face cream, hair, hairnets, powder, beads and old dust; that the blankets and flannelette sheets were unfresh; that there was no attempt at cheer or colour in the room; that in short, everything was uniformly dingy and need not be so. (pp. 7–8)

On the other hand, Mrs. Emblem's cheerful, sensuous, life-affirming presence is obviously expressed in her room:

> It was a room with a small ell. The ell was divided from the main part of the room by long rose-coloured curtains which at once suggested a delicious though precarious

privacy, an unravished something. How pleasant it was for Mrs. Emblem to go to bed behind those curtains, with her very fancy dressing table, made of a packing case and frilled by her own hands, beside her, a pinkly shaded light over her head, a rosy quilt upon the bed, the rose curtains open or drawn, the dying sounds of night passing up and down Burrard Street in the dark, some chocolates near at hand, a pink or blue dressing jacket loosely upon her white shoulders, her curls for tomorrow tied prettily within a pink or blue silken scarf finished with a knot or a bow, and the newspaper in her hands, opened at the Personal Column. (pp. 48–49)

But attention to detail and atmosphere in the setting of the novel is by no means confined to interiors. There is a continuous sense of the presence of Vancouver's streets, bridges, public buildings, wharves, inlet and river, surrounding mountains, over-arching sky, and variable weather. Just as the characters are prevailingly drab, with stray touches of glory and horror, so is the setting. We are given a far from flattering picture of Vancouver's streets and climate. Some of the descriptions of Vancouver approach the nature of set-pieces, but although they have touches of beauty they are by no means of the tourist brochure type:

So all of this did not trouble Morty very much as he bounced along through the outskirts of the sprawling city of Vancouver and looked out of the car windows at the soft grey day, day soft and damp and enervating, air opaque and lethargic, holding promise of rain. The handsome mountains which line the northern sky of Vancouver receive the impact of bodies of air travelling across from the Pacific Ocean, down from the Queen Charlotte Islands, down from the Aleutians, and these bodies of air, striking the handsome mountains, grow heavy, and sullen with increase; they break, and the rain falls and falls, and newcomers from the bright prairies wonder if they won't go back home if there's one more day of this rain, but oldtimers of Vancouver, though a little weary of the rain, know always that when a glorious day breaks on the green gound and on the mountains, this rain will be forgotten in the brilliant air. (pp. 96–97)

This attention to weather is one of the most unusual features of the novel. Never have I read a novel, except perhaps Hemingway's *A Farewell to Arms* and Dickens' *Bleak House,* in which I was so constantly made conscious of climatic conditions. The novel opens on a sunny morning, takes us through a hot day to a dark night; the second day begins dull, becomes increasingly wet and dark, and ends in a downpour in which we see a housewife taking in her sopping clothes "in the ill-lit darkness." (p. 129)

E. *Symbolic Values*

There is so much attention to light and darkness that these references take on symbolic value. Since Mrs. Wilson has expressed her suspicion of the symbol-hunting method of novel-reading, I hesitate to emphasize this aspect of her work. But in this novel, as in *Swamp Angel,* it is impossible to ignore the symbolic elements. The novel begins with "the fresh light of the rising sun" (p. 3) and ends with "the ill-lit darkness." (p. 129) On almost every page there are references to light and dark, and particularly in the second half of the novel these are almost always to lights of human origin struggling to illuminate the darkness of nature. Here are a few examples:

> The sun, at that time of the year, goes down suddenly, and then it is night before you know it. Pork began turning lights on in various places and this of itself changed the autumn afternoon into night in a funeral home. (p. 39)

> She [Vicky] likes to go to a show in one of the big movie houses on Granville Street where all the neon lights are. (p. 72)

> She [Vicky again] felt around in the darkness and found the electric light bulb hanging small and naked in the middle of the room. (p. 76)

> Eddie took a lunge in his story and stepped off the dark wharf into the dark night and fell with a tremendous splash into the dark water which closed over him and only a dirty spangly light moved on the surface of the water. . . . (p. 112)

> Victoria May, having no umbrella, walked in her rather

mincing way through the now driving rain and the darkness
and the occasional lights of Cordova Street along the black
and shining splashing pavements where a few people were
hurrying through the wet. (p. 127)

In the language of symbolism, light is traditionally equated with
the spirit, and is the manifestation of morality, the intellect, and
the virtues; it is also the creative force, cosmic energy, irradia-
tion, and spiritual strength. Darkness, on the other hand, is
associated with chaos, nihilism, the principle of evil. It seems
certain that Mrs. Wilson had these symbolic associations in
mind: her novel shows us the human spirit attempting to maintain its light amidst the surrounding darkness of the destructive
and death-dealing forces.

Closely related always to the symbolism of light and darkness
is the symbolism of colour. Again it is hard to believe that there
is not a more or less conscious of colour symbolism in *Tuesday
and Wednesday*. Mrs. Emblem is always golden, and her room
is predominantly pink; now gold, being the colour of the sun,
is symbolically associated with intuition, creativity, and with the
fertility of harvest, and pink, the colour of the flesh, is associated
with sensuality and the emotions: the aptness of all this to Mrs.
Emblem is clear. (And does not her very name suggest to us
her symbolic or emblematic character? She is the embodiment
of the feminine or maternal principle.) Mort Johnson, on the
other hand, from the opening reference to his grey blankets, is
always associated with the colour grey—and grey, the colour
of ashes, is symbolically expressive of depression, inertia, indifference and grief. The other colour frequently used in the
novel is blue: Mrs. Emblem wears a pink or blue dressing-jacket
and a pink or blue silken scarf, and she has grey-blue eyes;
Mort chooses a coffin lined with shining blue; Mrs. Lemoyne,
Myrt's employer, receives a blue handbag for her birthday; Eddie
Hansen is so fatally anxious to recover his suitcase because it
contains his bright blue suit. Blue, because of its association
with the sky, with Jupiter and Juno, and with the Virgin Mary,
stands for religious feeling, devotion, and innocence. It is its
innocence which is chiefly evoked here—the innocence of Mrs.
Emblem, the innocence of Mort's mood in the funeral parlour,
the innocent happiness of Mrs. Lemoyne's birthday, the lost
innocence for which Eddie Hansen is searching.

To this discussion of the symbols in the novel, we may conveniently append a discussion of the imagery. As is usual in Mrs. Wilson's work, the majority of the images are drawn from nature, especially animate nature. The instability of Mort's temperament is compared to "a rough mountainous sea" (p. 4); Vicky is compared to "some poor dawg that nobody wants" (p. 7); Mrs. Dunkerley is a bird that "came twittering, flying, across the grass" (p. 28); disturbing thoughts "turned themselves round and round like dogs settling down and then they settled to sleep" (p. 37); Vicky is compared to an anonymous fly, (p. 66) her voice to that "of a small twittering bird," (p. 95) and her eyes to black stars (p. 122); and people pass by in the dark, wet streets "silent as fishes," they "swam noiselessly past and vanished." (p. 89) The function of most of these images is to establish a harmony between man and the other parts of creation, to suggest that they are subject to a common happiness and a common fate.

But in this novel there is an unusual group of images—unusual, that is, in the work of Mrs. Wilson. These are images of an oriental or mythological sort. Mrs. Dunkerley is compared to a female Ganymede, (p. 15) Mrs. Emblem to "the jewel in the dark ear of the Ethiope," Vicky to a "fakir who has for so long held his arm unused that it is now atrophied." (p. 67) The function of these images, I suggest, is first of all to accentuate by contrast the drabness of the characters, setting, and plot of the novel, and secondly, on deeper consideration, to cause us to consider the extraordinary and magical qualities that even these seemingly ordinary people possess.

F. *Thematic Patterns*

Such considerations of meaning lead us to an examination of the themes of the novel. As usual, title and epigraph are clues. Tuesday and Wednesday: these are the most ordinary days of the week, without either the freshness of the beginning or the relief of the ending. The novel thus announces itself as a study of the ordinary, as an analysis of life on its most routine and everyday level. This, Mrs. Wilson seems to be saying, is what ordinary people are like—selfish, self-indulgent, lonely, vulnerable, changeable, but capable of moments of love, compassion and even an odd kind of heroism—and this is what ordinary life is like, a mixture of large parts of boredom and small parts of horror and glory. (The horror comes in with the coffins on pp. 40-41, the glimpse of Vicky's loneliness on pp. 67-68, and Eddie's and Mort's fall into the harbour on pp. 112-14; the glory with Vicky's story of Mort's heroism, with Mrs. Emblem's consolation of Myrtle, and the glimpse of religious exaltation in the description of the interior of St. James' Church on pp. 93-94.)

The epigraph on "Terewth" from *Bleak House*, quoted earlier, suggests a secondary theme: the novel is in one sense a demonstration of the difficulty of establishing the truth of ordinary human relations, even in a spirit of love. How, for example, can we be sure of the truth of Mort's character, when he is the ideal, experienced gardener one minute, and the lazy rebellious hired man the next? This point is suggested in relation to every character in the novel—only Mrs. Emblem and the kitten, types of innocence, are consistent throughout—and is made explicitly once: "People are very deceiving and you never can tell." (p. 31) Vicky sees Myrt and Mort "as kindly, chivalrous, handsome, elegant and an ideal couple" (p. 25); on other occasions they appear irascible, selfish, dingy, and quarrelsome; but which is the true view of them? No wonder Mrs. Dunkerley ruminates "how little we know about each other." (p. 30) A little boy disappears through a trap door, and a truculent man takes his place: which is the true Mort? And what is the truth about Mort's fall into the harbour? Was it an involuntary blunder, or a deliberate effort to save his friend's life? What is the truth about Mrs. Emblem's room?

> It is easy to be funny about the furniture-store romantic appearance of Mrs. Emblem's room, and for Myrtle to say that it is pink like a bad house. But it is not a bad house; it is a good house although it is only one room, and it is as much part of the essential Mrs. Emblem as her crinkly smile or her pink dressing gown. (p. 50)

If only real people were as simple and clean-cut as the characters in the funny papers! When Mrs. Emblem is reading the funnies, Mrs. Wilson comments:

> too difficult for those who read about Annie. Look at the new

character who makes his abrupt appearance in the picture. The lines of his jaw, his brow, at once disclose good or evil. You know exactly where you are: would that one's own acquaintance were so marked. (p. 54)

In real life you can never tell:

> When Eddie was sober and wore his overcoat with a velvet collar he did not look like a high rigger, bold and strong, magnificent among men, a rollicking Paul Bunyan of the Canadian woods, which he was; but like an imitation deacon, which he was not. (p. 87)

In spite of the clues given to us by the title and the epigraph, however, I feel that the deepest theme of the novel is the one suggested by the symbols and images. The predominant symbols, as we have seen, are those of light and darkness, and the predominant images those which link man with nature.

There is a beauty and rhythm in the natural universe—the beauty of colour, shape, and texture, the rhythm of day and night, light and dark, sunshine and rain—and man can share and delight in these things; but in the final analysis nature is indifferent to man, and at moments positively malignant. We read of Victoria May:

> As she hurried along the dark wet pavements, life and time continued as usual everywhere under heaven with practised ease their ceaseless fluid manipulations and arrangements of circumstance and influence and spiked chance and decision among members of the human family. . . . (p. 127)

There is throughout the novel a sense of a malignant fate at work, a fate that impels Eddie and Mort to that moment when they drown struggling in one another's arms. At such moments man is powerless against the forces of darkness—against "the dark wharf" and "the dark night" and "the dark water" he can oppose only "a dirty spangly light." (p. 112) But there is something positive in the theme of the novel at this level, a kind of subdued humanism. Men cannot conquer, and indeed they are too full of faults to deserve a full triumph, but they do achieve a kind of honour in defeat by displaying, at moments of real crisis, compassion, courtesy, and courage.

There is, then, an element of humanism. Is there also a touch
of Christianity, a genuinely Christian humanism? This is an aspect
of Mrs. Wilson's work about which I never feel quite sure. Our
attention is quite definitely drawn to the Christian context of
faith in this novel in the description of the exterior of St. James
Church, with its aery cross held up against the sky, (p. 93) and
more movingly in the subsequent description of the church's interior:

> The church, although barren of ornament, is not barren of
> beauty. It is cool, with a lovely austerity. There are six tall
> shining candlesticks at the altar. The candles are lighted.
> Seven small shining lamps hang suspended, their length of
> suspension forming pleasing curves which the eye follows
> gratefully and again follows. The shining lamps and their
> small ruby-shaded flames canalize the thought, the prayer,
> the dream. Then there is the large suspended crucifix, again
> aery; two plain pulpits; nothing more. The music accords
> with this, in pure and sweet enunciation. The services are
> ceremonial and also informal; man speaks to man; man lis-
> tens; God speaks to man through man in easy words that
> Vicky can understand, although she does not always listen;
> but she dreams, her eyes following the line of the suspended
> ruby flames of the seven shining lamps—up, down, up, down,
> up. Vicky does not know what all the short ceremonial of
> the service signifies, but it satisfies her, and she is aware,
> quite humbly, that it signifies something, or Father White-
> head would not perform it. (pp. 93-94)

Is there meant also to be a suggestion that Mort is a kind of
crucified Christ in the description of him before he plunges into
the water to join his friend? Here is the passage, with the passages italicized which seem to me to suggest some parallel with
Jesus on the Cross:

> Everything in the world narrows down now with horrid im-
> mediacy and intensity to only Eddie struggling alone down
> there in the dark and churning up the spangly water and
> clawing the empty water in panic haste because he cannot
> swim, and only Mort crouched *alone up there in the dark
> . . . in the sky it seems . . . his arms extended,* looking down
> into the high tide water under the dim light at the place

where Eddie churns his way up to the surface of the water. Everything in the world vanishes, gives way, all laughing and story give way to Mortimer's terror as, crouched *with his arms extended* as if frozen there, he sees the dark agitation of the water with its dirty spangled light and then he sees the white face of Eddie, staring, unrecognizable in its surprised fear, rise for a moment above the indifferent moving water. And at the sight of this white patch of face turning, choking, shouting, covered again, sinking again *Mort is vicariously in Eddie there*; he is Eddie, struggling there. (p. 113)

Is perhaps not the theme of the novel, at its deepest level, that man most fully achieves his humanity, in the face of "the indifferent moving water," when he imitates, however poorly and awkwardly, the self-sacrificial love of Christ?

G. *Techniques*

The novel's technique has all of Mrs. Wilson's strengths, and rather more than its share of her faults. To get the faults out of the way first, there are irritating and distracting examples of Mrs. Wilson's tendency to fall at times into a kind of self-conscious archness. The references to Mort's and Myrt's "angels" are one example; and the embarrassing "Woe for Mort. Woe for Mort's angel speeding away with an inaudible cry," (p. 114) which follows his drowning, is another. Similar are Mrs. Wilson's occasional authorial intrusions into the narrative: "I am sorry to say that it was Mr. H. Y. Dunkerley," (p. 31) "No one has seen Mrs. Emblem lying luxuriously there; but I see her now, and she looks so nice, she makes me feel good." (p. 49) Less irritating, but slightly unsettling, are the occasional set-pieces of biography, such as that of Horace Dunkerley on page 32, and of Vicky on page 64, and the unnecessary coincidences, such as Mort's discovery that he had known Dunkerley as a boy in Cape Breton Island. (p. 34)

But the strengths predominate. The prose style has Mrs. Wilson's usual unpretentious naturalness and ease, her unobtrusive handling of the colloquial and the idiomatic. Time is manipulated with her usual skill: the novel occupies two full days, two cycles from dawn through noon to night, and by unobtrusive

references to effects of light and shade and temperature Mrs.
Wilson makes us aware but not overly conscious of the flow
of the hours. One special feature of temporality here is the curious tacking effect achieved by having the beginning of one chapter go back to a time anterior to that with which the immediately
preceding chapter ended. (See, for example, the end of Chapter
XII and the beginning of Chapter XIII.) The overall structure
of the novel is very well managed: the novel opens at dawn and
closes at night; it begins with Mort getting out of bed and ends
with Victoria May going to bed; it begins in sunshine and ends
in rain.

For all its deceptive dreariness, there is much humour in the
novel. Mrs. Emblem refers to her two dead husbands (the third
was divorced) as her "two sod cases" (p. 23) and Mort's friend
Mr. Mottle is very amusing about doctors, patients, diseases and
tapeworms (pp. 102 ff.). The best passages of humour, however,
refer to the stray kitten, which wanders through the second half
of the novel as a symbol of saving and surviving innocence. But
if the kitten is a symbol, it is also a very real kitten, as the following delightful passage will reveal:

> The kitten, who was not a tom, felt her way about in the
> dark which was, to her, transparent, and learned the room.
> Feral, wise, with her inscrutable little hunter's nose and
> whiskers she felt and explored and recorded each chair leg,
> each table leg, each corner. She prowled and prowled on
> silent paws, and sometimes she stopped to wash. When she
> was satisfied, she accepted and adopted the room. Then she
> slept fitfully. She slept anywhere, lightly yet deeply, waking
> and moving often. Chiefly she slept on Mort and Myrtle
> who lay deep in sleep, warm and approved by her. But some-
> times she awoke, remembering something pleasant. Then
> she jumped lightly down and ran to her box. She scrambled
> up the side of her box and sat down, quivering, still, looking
> into the transparent dark with bliss. (p. 63)

III   Lilly's Story

One's first inclination is to approach *Lilly's Story* as primarily
a novel of character, the major interest and emphasis of which

is the constantly developing character of Lilly herself. Certainly
it is not a novel in which plot plays a major part. The outlines
of Lilly's story are quickly told: daughter of drunken and irresponsible parents who is cared for by a neighbour, she runs away
in her early teens to Vancouver and becomes a waitress, is seduced
by Yow (the Chinese servant of the Hastings family whom we
met in *The Innocent Traveller*), is in danger of police arrest because she has accepted stolen goods from her Chinese lover, runs
away again, to Nanaimo, where she lives with and becomes pregnant by a dark Welsh miner called Ranny Griffiths, bears an
illegitimate daughter Eleanor and goes to the Vancouver Island
village of Comox as a servant to Major and Mrs. Butler, runs
away from them when she realizes that her daughter will never
be anything but "the maid's daughter," becomes housekeeper in
a hospital in the Fraser Valley, runs away from there when Yow
reappears as the hospital cook, goes to Toronto, works as a
chambermaid, and meets and marries an elderly Winnipeg
widower, Mr. Sprockett. The plot thus is a simple chronological
and biographical one: there is an obvious resemblance to Defoe's
Moll Flanders, but Lilly is much more briefly licentious than Moll,
much more responsible as a mother, and much more industrious
as a person, and there are hardly any of the coincidences, accidental reappearances, and mistakes of identity which complicate
the plot of Defoe's novel. The only accidental reappearance is
that of Yow, and the melodramatic possibilities of that event are
deliberately played down: Lilly never actually confronts him, but
simply sees him through her window and leaves the place at
once. Indeed so lacking is the novel in conventionally exciting
plot devices and patterns that it led a *New Yorker* reviewer, in
virtually the only hostile review that the book received, to describe
it as "an inertly written lesson on how to creep through life."[2]

Character, then, is more important than plot in *Lilly's Story*—
or indeed we might say that character is its plot. But even more
important than character, I believe, is the novel's theme. *Lilly's
Story* is apparently merely the simple life-story of a humble and
essentially simple woman; it is actually a powerful thematic novel
which, to put it briefly but much too crudely, illustrates the
eternally valid notion that "perfect love casteth out fear." It is
not so much a novel about one woman's life, as a novel about
love and fear, unity and separation, glory and horror.

A. *Thematic Patterns*

I am persuaded to see *Lilly's Story* as primarily a novel of theme rather than of character because the single most memorable element in it is not Lilly, deeply moving as she is, but the great central scene in which Lilly and her daughter witness a kitten in pursuit of a robin, a robin in pursuit of a snake, an eagle in pursuit of the kitten, and a gull and a crow in pursuit of the eagle. The scene, too long to quote in full, concludes with this paragraph:

> The kitten did not see the eagle whose shadow had now twice passed over it. The robin did not see the kitten who had lain quivering from nose to tail not five feet way. The eagle did not see two enemies who now assailed him from the rear. From the sky swooped a gull and from the fir trees on the near shore flew a crow; white bird and black bird, inveterate enemies of the eagle, came to beat him away from their homes and children. Lilly held fast the kitten who lashed its angry tail. At this moment the robin, successfully gathering the snake together in two loops, rose heavily and flew low and away, unaware of kitten or eagle, woman or child. The battle now remained between the two birds and the eagle. The hunt of robin for snake, cat for robin, eagle for cat was over. (Everything after something, thought Lilly.) With harsh cries the white and black birds beat about the great and ancient bird's flanks and tail, manoeuvring quickly. The eagle could not swiftly turn, and continued its majestic soaring at quicker speed. The gull and the crow beat about its tail crying loudly until it seemed to Lilly that the crow was exhausted. It flew to a spindling broken tree while the gull continued the attack. Then the crow returned, followed by more crows from the fir trees, and the seagull flapped away towards the shore, ejaculating from time to time as seagulls do. The crows beat violently about the rear of the eagle who retreated, still circling, and became somewhere invisible as eagles do. The crows returned, praising themselves loudly, as crows do. The hunt was over and only the small garter snake had perished. Around and about among the grasses a myriad invisible hunts went on. I wisht

another grown-up person had been here to see that, Lilly reflected, still looking into the distance, that was the queerest thing I ever did see in all my life. She felt uneasy . . . seems like everything's cruel, hunting something. (pp. 191-93)

At least two of the major themes of the novel are symbolically or actually present in that scene.

First of all, there is the sense, found abundantly also in *Tuesday and Wednesday*, of the variability and ambiguity of life. The passage we have just quoted is preceded by a paragraph describing the idyllic beauty of the day:

On this glorious day the sky seemed higher and wider than usual. The vault was blue and of intense clarity. A large tumble of white cumulus lay motionless near the horizon. . . . On this fair day of summer the fresh loveliness of the place with a light breeze blowing brought Lilly one of those perfect moments of time that seem to last forever. . . . (p. 191)

Out of the midst of this innocence and purity—notice how here again Mrs. Wilson appears to have used the colours of blue and white symbolically—comes the horror of the hunt. The kitten is an "innocent creature" one moment, and the next is "transformed to a ruthless hunting cat." (pp. 191-92)

Secondly, and more important, there is the sense of life as a truly fearful process, a perpetual pursuit of the hunted by the hunter. There is the fear of impermanence: "those perfect moments . . . do not last forever, and are so fleeting that they make some people afraid." And there is the more intense fear of physical violence: "the little snake slid, coiled, lashed out." Inevitably we proceed to associate the snake with Lilly: throughout the major portion of the novel we see *her* sliding, coiling, lashing out. We realize that images of fear, and images of the hunter and the hunted, interweave as thematic motifs throughout the book. Yow, the Chinese cook, appears as both predator and prey: "He admitted that, in China, he had killed two men, one slowly, one quickly. He also said that he had been beaten to within an inch of his life." (p. 174) When the police are on the trail of the stolen goods, Lilly is likened to a hunted animal: "Lilly crouched, turned, and ran . . . crouching in the shadows, listening, hardly daring to look behind her." (pp. 144-45) When Lilly hears her mother and her mother's lover coming to look

for her, she runs away like a cat. (p. 147) When she is trying to
hide the stolen goods she has received from Yow, we are told
that "she looked about her like one hunted," (p. 159) and later,
in Nanaimo, her Welsh lover Ranny is described as "a kennel into
which a homeless worthless bitch crawls." (p. 164) At Comox,
Lilly's daughter Eleanor confronts a wildcat in the woods:

> And there, in the middle of the silent open glade sat a great
> cat with beards on his chin and a strong tuft of hair on the
> end of each of his ears. He sat proudly in the sun, owning
> the world. The animal's large lambent eyes, each slitted with
> black, gazed into the forest. Then the eyes closed and the
> cat opened its mouth wide in a silent cry. The little child
> stepped out into the sunny glade, her arms by her side and
> her fingers spread. She stumbled and looked down. She
> looked up, and the great cat had gone. She had not heard
> him go, but the glade was empty. (p. 171)

At the Fraser Valley hospital, fear is expressed in the image of a
steel trap: "But about and behind her spread always her intangible and invisible Then, solid as steel, inescapable as past
birth or death to come." (p. 222) Lilly, like the hunted snake,
lashes out when Paddy tries to make love to her: "as he tried to
take her again she struck him across the face in a frenzy of fear."
(p. 226) When Yow reappears as the hospital cook, Lilly draws
back "into the shade of her kitchen curtains like a silent animal
withdrawing into the cover of the forest." (p. 242) The trap
image recurs on page 244: "It's like I was in a trap," Lilly thinks.
Three pages later she is coiling to escape like the snake: "she
dodged again, she lied again, and felt no guilt." In Toronto, Lilly
is compared to a frightened deer: "A deer in the city . . . see the
sabled delicate deer startled on the edge of the multitude . . . the
voices of the multitude startle the delicate elegant deer. . . ." (p.
267)

The words "fear," "afraid," "fright" or "frightened" appear at
least once on at least thirty-five pages of this short novel, and
almost until the very last page Lilly feels herself in danger. She
is always on the run; her life is a series of escapes. She runs away
from her parents, her foster-mother, Yow, the police, Ranny
Griffiths, the Butlers, Mrs. Meakins, Paddy, and the hospital. She
is always afraid: afraid of her parents, her lover, the police, her

foster-mother; afraid of being recognized in Vancouver, afraid of the discovery of Eleanor's illegitimacy, afraid of Mr. Sprockett finding out that she is wearing a wig, afraid of her past rising up to spoil her present. Again and again we see her as a hunted being:

> Running, stopping, running again down the dark lanes and alleys, and walking, tense and with quickly beating heart across the lighter streets, she hunted wildly within herself, doubling and twisting, for some means of getting away at once from the unexpected terror which had only a few minutes ago sprung at her and entangled her. She did not need anyone to tell her that her presents from Yow had been stolen and that she was wearing stolen goods at that moment. She knew it instinctively from the clamour at the box-room door and she feared everything for herself. She feared only for herself. She gave Yow no thought at all, save for the terror that he might set the police on her. (p. 157)

Only at the end of the book, when her devoted love has established the security of her daughter, now married to a Vancouver lawyer, and of herself, about to marry Mr. Sprockett, can she feel "She would be without fear; nothing, surely, could touch her now." (p. 277)

Closely related to fear is loneliness, the sense of isolation, and references to this are almost as frequent. When Lilly leaves her foster-mother, Mrs. Case, we are told that "she was alone. . . . No one had loved her, and she did not even know that she had missed love." (p. 156) When she discovers that she is pregnant we read:

> She dared not write to any friend in Vancouver. She had no friend in Vancouver. She had no friend anywhere in the world. . . . She trusted no one and was quite alone. (p. 168)

On her way to the Butlers' at Comox, she is described as "a poor young widow alone in the world." (She is not really a widow, but she pretends to be, and takes the name Mrs. Walter Hughes). After the angry scene with Paddy, the handyman at the hospital, we are told:

> She overflowed with a sad compassion both blind and dumb for Eleanor and for herself and then, as with discovery and

a melancholy surprise, for anyone anywhere who might suffer or be lonely as she was lonely. (P. 227)

When Yow's arrival forces Lilly to leave the hospital, she weeps "at the thought of leaving those who were her life"—she "wept painfully, and wept hopelessly, and wept alone." (p. 245) On her lonely train journey to Toronto, we are told that "She felt the strange taste of sorrow in her throat, and in her stomach the cold core of lead that only the desolate know," (p. 248) and in Toronto itself she is "desperately lonely." (p. 250)

Lilly's loneliness is matched by that of Mr. Sprockett. After his first wife's death, he "could not bear to be alone, and he knew it." (p. 258) His home now seems desolate:

> In two days' time Mr. Sprockett would board the train and go west to Winnipeg and open up the house whose air was lifeless and depleted. Once a week there were the signs that the cleaning woman had been there. But when he went home at night never a thing was stirring in that house, empty from wall to wall. Never a sound from the kitchen, never the long telephone conversation with "the girls" about bridge, never the shrieks of laughter. . . . He was not moping exactly but his empty house was desolate. (pp. 260-61)

He awakes each morning "into emptiness and silence, alone in the bed, the room, the house, the void." (p. 272)

The remedy for both fear and loneliness is love, and since Mrs. Wilson is not the sort of author to give an entirely negative and bleak view of life, she provides the remedy in many forms. Even Yow is capable of love, love of two very different sorts:

> He was mad over Lilly. He was mad over old Mrs. Hastings too. Two different loves. He loved Mrs. Hastings steadily, purely, and disliked all other white people on principle. His love for Lilly was a desire that consumed him. . . . (p. 137)

"Love," then, means many things, and is not necessarily good. There is the love which gives, and the love which takes, and only the former is permanently valuable. Lilly's mother and her lodger are in love, but their love consists in drinking and quarrelling between bouts of sensuality, and leads them to desert the woman's only child. Lilly's love for Yow is selfish love: she goes

with him only because he gives her expensive presents. Her love
for Ranny Griffiths, the Welsh miner in Nanaimo who fathers
her child, is equally selfish: she lives with him because "It seemed
the easiest thing to do," (p. 161) goes to him as to "a kennel into
which a homeless worthless bitch crawls." (p. 164)

But even within the broad category of the love which gives,
there are distinctions to be made. Lilly's love for her daughter
Eleanor is altruistic, but it is for a long time merely instinctive
and undiscriminating:

> Lilly's whole body and spirit which had never known a
> direction, were now solely directed towards giving Baby
> everything that Lilly could give her. Lilly never said to
> herself, "I want Baby to have everything I have never had."
> Nothing was relative to the past. She said, instead, "Baby
> shall have everything I can get her. Baby must be like folks."
> (p. 173)

And so, ruled by mere instinct, "Lilly would lie (for Baby) if
need be (as she had lied her own way along her life) and
she would steal for Baby as long as she would not be discovered."
(p. 174) As the novel proceeds, Lilly learns the real nature of
selfless and intelligent love: from this point of view *Lilly's Story*
might be sub-titled "A Sentimental Education." She learns, for
example, to blend "with her worship of the child a good deal of
shrewdness and hardness, keeping Eleanor well in hand." (p. 183)
She learns, too, to think of Eleanor not only as a mere "part of
her [self]" (p. 173) but as a separate individual, who need not
be either like her mother or like other people:

> But sometimes even Lilly, looking down on the sleeping
> Eleanor, would think Can this be my baby? She's a lady,
> that's what she is. She's not common. She's better than
> folks, she's like she was Mrs. Butler's kid. I'm not so com-
> mon neither as I was. I guess I've learned a bit. (p. 188)

And, out of her increasingly selfless love for her daughter, she
learns to control her own temptation to indulge in casual, sensual
love-making. Mr. Butler, her employer's husband, makes over-
tures to her, but she resists (as she had not resisted Yow or
Ranny):

Well, now he had tested her; but the girl was so stupid
that he let her alone, irritated with himself that he could be
stirred by anything so dull. But Lilly was not dull, and she
said to herself The silly fool, what does he take me for? If
it had not been for Eleanor she would have accepted his
understood invitation, she would have played. . . . (p. 189)

This lesson stands her in good stead when, at the Fraser Valley
hospital, she is tempted by the sentimental, urgent, but shallow
passion of Mr. Meakins, the elderly Chairman of the Hospital
Board. Mr. Meakins exhibits another "equation of love":

On the Sundays that Mrs. Hughes and her little girl were
at church, Mr. Meakins looked at the straight back of Lilly
Waller who was Mrs. Walter Hughes, and the turmoil in his
mind increased and maddened him. He could not take his
eyes from the form of Mrs. Hughes, and on the alternate
Sundays, when she was not there, he pictured her there,
standing, kneeling, bowed in prayer—what prayer? His blood
began to tell him so loudly about this woman that he was
afraid that people would see, that they would hear, and that
he would betray himself. He had fallen in love with a green
tweed back. He became sentimental, and he knew it. I'm
crazy, he said to himself, and what can I do? (p. 213)

Lilly meets this challenge with a dignity and a deliberation which
reveal how much she has matured since she was a silly girl accepting stolen stockings and panties from Yow:

After Eleanor was in bed that evening, Lilly put the question to herself. If I wanted to, I guess I could marry him,
she thought, not right now maybe, but go along quietly and
mind my own business and I could marry him. Lilly, sitting
by her fire, considered. She weighed the matter coolly and
found that she would not marry Mr. Meakins and that she
could make that apparent to Mr. Meakins as easy as easy
without making talk. (pp. 216-17)

As for Mr. Meakins, "Having been thus for a time deranged by
love, he married somebody else shortly afterwards."

Lilly also learns that love can be something quite different from
either sexual passion or maternal love. The relationship between

Lilly and the Matron is based on companionship and mutual respect:

> Between the Matron and Lilly was that relation that exists a few times in some fortunate lives where there is mutual respect and affection and a real though limited pleasure in companionship, with which relative education has little to do. Lilly was ignorant. The Matron was a woman of some education, intuitive, quick-witted, practical, but with a joy in beauty and an unsatisfied aesthetic taste beyond anything that Lilly could ever know. She still stayed in the Valley where aesthetic pleasures were in part denied her because she loved the claims of her work and her people. She had become a personage in her own place. Not beautiful, hardly good-looking, she got on well with men and women. The Matron had come to mean to Lilly everything that Lilly respected or could wish to be. She was the only person with the exception of Eleanor for whom Lilly had ever felt any sentiment of affection. On the Matron's part, Lilly's solitary condition, her independence, her uncompromising devotion to her child and to her work, aroused the older woman's protection and, perhaps, her curiosity. Where I love, I meddle, mused the Matron, and she did. She loved the child, watched her, and corrected her. (pp. 218-19)

But Lilly is not yet secure. Her greatest temptation to substitute the love that takes for the love that gives comes from Paddy Wilkes. He is married, has several children, but he is very susceptible and very attractive. Again it is her now quite selfless love for Eleanor that saves her:

> Now, each day, she looked for him, she needed him, and he who had seemed to be almost hers was not hers any longer. He belonged to nobody, to everybody, and to his shadowy family who lived somewhere beyond the village. She knew that what she felt for him she had never yet felt for any man. To Lilly it passed for love.
>
> For a very short time she was happy in her secret way. Her love was as when a fruit is opened, and the scent flows out like a wine, never as sweet again. But soon she asked herself Well, what of it? What could she do? There was nothing in

it for her, and then the sweetness was gone. If it had not been for Eleanor and for the life that Lilly had arranged for Eleanor (and so for herself) she would have set herself to seduce Paddy if she could, and perhaps she could. At least she would not have been scrupulous. She thought a little scornfully He's easy . . . a woman's only got to give a sign. She would have made talk and trouble but she would not have cared much, and she could have moved on. But about and behind her spread always her intangible and invisible Then, solid as steel, inescapable as past birth or death to come, making her Now always insecure and always scrupulous—for Eleanor. Thus, since her birth, the child Eleanor, all unknowing, had guarded her mother and had made her the blameless and silent woman that she had become, who now was crushing out her love. (pp. 221-22)

When Paddy actually touches her, she momentarily yields, but the thought of Eleanor sustains her. This episode, rather than the subsequent reappearance of Yow, is the real climax of the story. Lilly has mastered the lust, selfishness, and greed that marked her early character, and has learned self-control and compassion. Her love from now on goes beyond herself, beyond her daughter, to all suffering humanity:

> She overflowed with a sad compassion both blind and dumb for Eleanor and for herself and then, as with discovery and a melancholy surprise, for anyone anywhere who might suffer or be lonely as she was lonely. (p. 227)

But Lilly's education in love is not yet complete. She selflessly allows Eleanor to go off to Vancouver to train as a nurse, and there Eleanor falls in love with and marries the young lawyer, Paul Lowry. Visiting her daughter and her son-in-law, Lilly witnesses an equation of love hitherto unknown to her:

> One afternoon Lilly came out of her bedroom door, moving quietly as usual, just as Paul came in and ran up the stairs. He ran up calling "Nora!" and Eleanor came quickly out of their bedroom. They did not see Lilly, but Lilly, standing in her doorway, saw Eleanor come up to her husband with her face raised, and on her face a revealed look that Lilly had never seen on Eleanor's face nor on any face. Eleanor's face

was changed and radiant. For a moment the husband and wife looked at each other. They did not speak. Then they kissed. Paul remained with his arms around his wife and his face to hers. They were alone, and this moment had revealed their felicity. What was it all about? All that had happened was that Paul had come home to dinner. Was there some special secret life that these two led together, of which other people had no knowledge? There was. Of that Lilly felt sure, as, quickly, having seen what she had seen, she stepped back into her room and quietly closed the door. She sat down on her bed, shaken by her daughter's look. She had lived for nearly fifty years, and she had never seen this thing before. So this was love, each for each, and she had never known it. And this secret life of love went on in this house and she had never seen it before. She was outside it. (p. 239)

Quite this degree of felicity, or rapture, Lilly is never to experience in her own person, although I think we are meant to assume that this glimpse of it will enrich her final relationship with Mr. Sprockett. But we are told that Mr. Sprockett lived for thirty-nine years with his first wife "not in rapture but in the perfect satisfaction which is one equation of love," (p. 257) and it is probable that it will be perfect satisfaction rather than rapture that he will have in his marriage with Lilly. However, if the relationship between Lilly and Mr. Sprockett is not quite "felicity," it is something remarkably close to it. In its early stages, their relationship is compared to a pleasant meadow-land:

Lilly and Mr. Sprockett had progressed last night into that pleasant stream-fed meadow-land in which men and women find themselves, where no names are used, a place of more or less magical anonymity which words do not describe. Sometimes you return to the street names and shop names of daily living. Less frequently, but sometimes in nearly every life, progress is made further into personally owned and fenced-in territory. (p. 273)

For Lilly, the marriage is basically self-less, primarily a matter of giving, and carefully pondered: "I can make him happy. . . ." (p. 275)

In this context, love "meant looking after him and thinking for him and guarding him from harm." (p. 277) But it is enough to cause Mr. Sprockett "so much rapture" (p. 277) and "Lilly was happy too, happier than she had even been." (p. 277) Love has cast out fear: "She would be without fear; nothing, surely, could touch her now." Love, too, has cast out falsehood: Lilly insists on telling him about her wig: "I wouldn't have liked to deceive you . . . I wouldn't want to have anything to hide." (p. 280) When Sprockett asks her which church she will be married in, Lilly replies, significantly, "United," speaking "almost inaudibly, faint with her happiness." (p. 281) And that is the novel's last word. We feel that Lilly and Mr. Sprockett are now indeed safe, that they have moved in to that "fenced-in territory" (p. 273) which is only vulnerable to death.

My mention of death is deliberate, for it would be quite wrong to suggest that the final message of this novel is a pollyanna optimism. It is a novel of constant tension, in which fear struggles with love, selfish love with unselfish love, the sense of alienation with the sense of belonging, a revulsion from the horror of life with an attraction to life's brief glories. Insofar as Lilly wins through at the end to happiness, the novel is affirmative, affirmative of a kind of stubborn humanism which manages to achieve a partial victory in the face of almost insuperable odds. But we should notice that the victory is only partial: Lilly is able to marry the man of her choice only when she is about fifty, and he well over sixty. The happiness they will share will not be for long.

B. *Symbolism*

There is, however, another dimension to the theme of the novel which we have not yet explored. *Lilly's Story* is not only about the growth of one human being from selfish irresponsibility to mature and selfless love, nor even about the difficulties and occasional triumphs of humanity in general. There is a metaphysical or at least superhuman dimension to it as well. The whole universe is seen as poised between opposites, between glory and horror. The images and symbols which reinforce the humanist theme also suggest this more universal theme. Nature, for example, is seen throughout the novel to wear a double face, to be now destructive, now consoling. The innocent kitten is transformed into the ruthless cat. The fierce wildcat which Eleanor confronts in the woods does not exercise its power, but withdraws gently in the face of the child's innocence. Against the beasts and birds of prey in the novel—the snake, the eagle, the crow, the wildcat—are set the gentle, friendly beasts, the dogs and kittens with which Eleanor plays, the deer to which Lilly is likened in Toronto, the frightened bitch crawling to its kennel. There are almost as many references to the healing power of inanimate nature: "the consolation of sea and wind and strange wooded shores," (p. 160) "the fresh loveliness of the place with a light breeze blowing," (p. 191) "scarves of mist and smoke . . . upon a landscape of golden poplars, dark conifers, broad meadows, cattle grazing there, the winding river reflecting forest and sky." (pp. 225-26) The suggestion seems to be that, although nature is neutral or indifferent towards man, there is in the natural world a "cycle" (Lilly's word for it, after she has watched the hunt of kitten for robin for snake, etc.) or rhythm, or order in apparent disorder, from the full realization of which man can find at least temporary release from his troubles. There is, in other words, implied a kind of natural mysticism, similar to that which Wordsworth expressed in "Tintern Abbey":

> On such a day as this and in such a place Eleanor would— some day and days—be aware of the incorporeal presence in air, and light, and dark, and earth, and sea, and sky, and in herself, of something unexpressed and inexpressible, that transcends and heightens ordinary life, and is its comple- ment. (p. 194)

That prophecy is fulfilled when Eleanor has grown to young womanhood:

> She was aware as time went on, without defining anything to herself, that her mother had little sense of humour and little of beauty. There is a wild disorder of nature which is beauty. Eleanor could see it and feel it and Lilly could not feel it at all. Eleanor did not often think of the time before they came to the Valley, but sometimes she was led to re- member the sand spit at Comox, with the wind blowing over, and the little headstones, and the bending grasses; she remembered the boat on a blue sea as still as glass, or toss- ing on grey white curling water, and she wanted to see the ocean again; she remembered a great cat in the sunlight in

an open glade, and its green lambent eyes; she remembered the elegance of a china horse and a china dog; she remembered vaguely stories told and books read aloud by Mrs. Butler, some she had understood, some she had not understood, but she had listened. (pp. 230-31)

The reference in that passage to "the elegance of a china horse and a china dog" leads us to another mystical strain in the novel, to what might be called the mysticism of art. Here the connection is not with Wordsworth, but with Keats's "Ode on a Grecian Urn." When Lilly first arrives at the Butler home at Comox, the horse and dog are described thus:

Above the mantelpiece of a neat open grate in which no fire burned was a large mirror framed in gilt. Lilly looked wonderingly at this. Towards one end of the mantelpiece were two ancient pieces of Chinese pottery, a hound and a horse. The melancholy hound, of a fair Chinese yellow glaze, held his head lifted as if listening for centuries for a master who did not come. Each elegant rib showed finely below the skin. The blue horse, standing beside the yellow hound, grazed peacefully forever where no grass grew, upon the shining mantelpiece. The hound and the horse were reflected in the shining mirror which held the room as in a picture. Two hounds and two horses. Soft broken light lay on the walls and on the dark shining floor. Everywhere was light or a dark shine. Light and shade falling through large vine leaves moving outside the window made moving pools of light and shade in this yellow room. Lilly's gaze returned to the hound and the horse, creatures detached from ordinary living, motionless yet somehow aware, in a world of their own. I'd be scared to touch them, she thought, I'd be scared to dust them. (p. 178)

These beautiful objects, which are referred to again five times in the novel (on pp. 181, 185, 203, 204, 231), are obviously symbols of an eternal beauty which dwells at the heart of life. But the beauty itself is antithetical, a tension of opposites: melancholy hound and happy horse, darkness and light, yellow (symbolic of intellect) and blue (symbolic of innocence and adoration). Behind the horse and hound, significantly, is the mirror, symbol of the imagination in its capacity to reflect the formal reality of the visible world, and of the world as thesis and antithesis.

C. *Characterization*

The foregoing has been, I hope, sufficient to demonstrate that *Lilly's Story* is a powerful thematic novel. It is also a triumph of characterization. Lilly is the least static of fictional characters: she goes from vacuous irresponsibility to mature self-devotion in a series of logical and emotionally valid stages. When we first see her, she is "a white girl with taffy-coloured hair" (p. 134) who is indifferent to everything except material values:

> . . . In her indifferent way Lilly played with him. She was not fastidious. She was not vicious. She was no particular good and she had an inordinate desire for *things*. (p. 137)

When we last see her she is "this perfect perfect woman" (p. 281) who is thinking not of things, not even of herself, but of making Mr. Sprockett happy, of making her daughter happy, of looking after the Matron. Such a complete change seems incredible; it is a tribute to the skill and artistic cunning of Ethel Wilson that she makes the process very credible indeed. Each time that Lilly speaks and acts, she speaks and acts in character, and yet each time there is a barely perceptible change. It is quite in keeping with her character, as it then was, that she should shamelessly give Yow a peep-show as she puts on the stockings he has stolen for her (p. 141); it is the same, but paradoxically a changed, Lilly who accepts for a moment and then angrily rejects the advances of Paddy Wilkes. The fires are still there but she has learned to bank them.

The characterization of Lilly, the subtlety of which we have only glanced at, is dependent for much of its success upon the clever but unobtrusive way in which Ethel Wilson suggests the passage of time. After all, thirty or thirty-five years is a long time-span for a novel of only about a hundred and fifty pages, and yet Mrs. Wilson never either lets us lose sight of passing time, or resorts to conventional formulae such as "ten years had passed" or the insertions of rows of dots or asterisks. By carefully but naturally noting the changes in Lilly's looks, speech habits, clothes, interests, and attitudes towards herself and others she makes us feel the reality and the inevitability of the passing days, weeks, months and years. It is done by a constant and unremitting attention to minute detail worthy of Jane Austen or Arnold Bennett.

D. *Techniques*

This minute attention to objective detail is perhaps the most conspicuous feature of the technique of "Lilly's Story." The coy, first personal intrusions by the author which occasionally marred Mrs. Wilson's earlier novels have all but disappeared. The whole fabric of the novel is closely interwoven of its own stuff. Even the set-pieces of description—descriptions of Vancouver, of the Canadian landscape—which were delightful in themselves in the earlier books, but which did somewhat impede the narrative flow, even these have been ruthlessly eliminated. When there are descriptions, with the single exception of the long symbolic passage concerning the cycle of the hunter and the hunted, they are brief, impressionistic, and seen through the eyes of the characters in the story. Mrs. Wilson has even denied herself, for artistic purposes, the luxury of humour. Since Lilly has "little sense of humour," (p. 230) there is almost no humour in the novel. (It may be that the final reference to the "United" Church is meant to suggest that Lilly is developing in this respect also. The literal meaning, of course, is the United Church of Canada, a union, dating from 1925, of Methodists, Congregationalists, and Presbyterians; but a pun seems intended: Lilly is at last to be truly "united" and not alone.)

The structure of *Lilly's Story* is almost wholly chronological, the only disorder in the time scheme being the return to Lilly's early childhood in Chapter 2, after her seduction by Yow in Chapter 1. Since the stages of Lilly's life hold the novel so firmly together, and move it so regularly forward, there is no need for other structural devices. The novel is arranged in twenty chapters which vary in length from three to fifteen pages; each chapter relates one significant episode in the life of Lilly or, near the end, the life of Mr. Sprockett. As is usual in Mrs. Wilson's work, each chapter is in a sense a complete unit, but cleverly integrated also with those that follow and precede it.

Lilly's Story is a minor triumph both as a work of art and as a human document. In one hundred and fifty pages it shows us the detailed development of a human soul, traces the essential outlines of a sentimental education, and presents us with the rhythmic pattern or cycle of hunter and hunted, darkness and light, fear and love, separation and unity—and all this through the medium of a girl who, when the novel begins, "was no particular good" and "had an inordinate desire for *things.*"

CHAPTER 6

Swamp Angel (1954)

ETHEL Wilson's capacity to make an interesting novel with cosmic implications out of a slight plot and apparently ordinary characters is nowhere better illustrated than in *Swamp Angel*.[1] By using every resource at the novelist's command—variations of tone and point of view, alternations between the panorama and the close-up, thematic images, self-analysis and cross-analysis of character, the symbolic employment of landscape and weather, for example—she succeeds in making this simple story into a parable of the whole human condition, of indeed, the whole cosmic rhythm and web. *Swamp Angel*, which seems on the face of it to be a story of a small group of people in British Columbia, is really, by implication at least, a prose poem about the cosmic web of life, about time and eternity, man's relations with God, virtually all aspects of man's relations with his fellows (parent and child, husband and wife, employer and employee, friendship and envy), the individual's struggle for survival in a universe which at least seems to be profoundly indifferent to him, and the relations of the animate creation with the inanimate.

I *Plot*

The plot may be quickly outlined. Maggie Vardoe, whose first husband had been killed in the War, leaves her second husband, Eddie Vardoe, determined to make a new life for herself. She accepts a job as cook and housekeeper for Haldar and Vera Gunnarsen, who have recently established a fishing lodge on Three Loon Lake, near Kamloops. She is very successful in this position, but she makes Vera jealous of her, and for a while it appears that the unpleasantness of this relationship will force her to give up the job. Vera makes a half-hearted attempt to commit suicide, and in her extremity it is Maggie who comforts her. The novel ends with Maggie and the Gunnarsens looking forward to a new season at the lodge, the suggestion being that Maggie will do all that she can—and it may not be enough—to nurse Vera back to full spiritual and physical health.

This is the main plot line, but beside it is a strong secondary plot involving Maggie's husband, Eddie, and her friends, Mrs. Severance and her daughter Hilda. When Maggie leaves Eddie, he is so angry that he thinks of killing her; it is a glimpse of Mrs. Severance's revolver, the so-called Swamp Angel, that dissuades him from this course, together with her worldly-wise advice to seek consolation in the company of some other young lady. Eddie eventually acquires a blonde mistress, Ireen, with whom he will be as happy as such a fundamentally weak man can ever hope to be. Mrs. Severance decides that her beloved revolver, the Swamp Angel, has become too important to her as a symbol of her past life, and she sends it to Maggie with instructions to hurl it in the lake whenever Mrs. Severance dies. In the last scene of the novel, Maggie performs this rite. Hilda Severance, meanwhile, who was a lonely and introverted young woman when the novel began, falls in love and marries in the course of it, and is a proud young mother at its close. Minor characters are the two young Chinese men, Joey and Angus, who act as Maggie's assistants and drivers at various times, the Gunnarsens' young son, Alan, and the Gunnarsens' friend in Kamloops, Henry Corder.

II *Characterization*

The first element which makes this novel much more richly significant than this plot outline would suggest is the subtlety and complexity with which its characters are developed. There is nothing flat or static about any of them, with the possible exception of Henry Corder. We see each of them through his own eyes, through the eyes of the other characters, and through Mrs. Wilson's eyes, so that for each of them we get a sense of a multiple personality, of a group of masks behind which we are forever trying to glimpse the essential person. Each of them de-

velops as the novel proceeds, and yet each step in his development can be seen to be the logical outcome of tendencies already
present.

Maggie Vardoe (or Maggie Lloyd, as she prefers to be called)
is in a sense another version of Lilly in *Lilly's Story*, of the self-
reliant woman who makes her own way in the world by sheer
will-power and determination. But she is quite distinct from
Lilly, for she has a much more intense response to her fellows.
Whereas Lilly's love was almost wholly confined to her daughter
and to her eventual husband, Maggie is truly compassionate
towards the Chinese boys, towards the Severances, and above all
to Vera Gunnarsen. She is, like Lilly, a victor rather than, like
Mort and Myrtle in *Tuesday and Wednesday*, a victim, but she
is a compassionate victor. And yet—and these qualifications suggest how complex her seemingly simple character is—there are
strict limits to her compassion. She had married Eddie Vardoe
out of compassion but eventually she leaves him almost ruthlessly:

> She had once lived through three deaths, and—it really
> seemed—her own. Her country had regretted to inform her
> that her husband, Tom Lloyd, was killed in action; their
> child was stricken, and died; and Maggie Lloyd, with no one
> to care for, had tried to save herself by an act of compassion
> and fatal stupidity. She had married Edward Vardoe. (p. 6)
> .   .   .
> . . . It's a good thing I'm going now, she thought as she
> stirred the gravy. I'm always unfair, now, to Edward. I
> hate everything he does. He has only to hang up his hat and
> I despise him. Being near him is awful. I'm unfair to him
> in my heart always whatever he is doing, but tonight I
> shall be gone. (p. 7)

Afterwards she feels occasional twinges of guilt about leaving
Eddie, but nothing changes her "private determination" (p. 15)
because her "endurance" has been "outraged." (p. 15)

The characterization of Maggie illustrates well Ethel Wilson's
emphasis on relativity, on the variant effects of the point of
view. Inwardly, to her own eye, Maggie is anxious and fearful:

> Her look and habit had not betrayed her although she
> had lived more and more urgently through the last few

weeks when an irrational fear had possessed her that she, or he, would become ill, would meet with an accident, that some car, some fall, some silly bodily ailment would, with the utmost indignity and indifference, interfere . . . (p. 2)

To Hilda Severance, however, she is "that calm, placid Maggie," (p. 42) Haldar Gunnarsen's plans for the future are based on "the steadiness of Maggie," (p. 150) and Henry Corder thinks of "the jewel of Maggie's integrity." (p. 154) Although to the Gunnarsens she appears as a victor and indeed as a saviour, to herself she appears as a failure:

> With all her fine talk and with all her high thinking she had not been able to cope with one unhappy human be-ing. . . . Human relations . . . how they defeat us. Yes, I am defeated. (p. 195)

This ambiguity extends even to her physical appearance. Mr. Spencer, to whose sporting goods store she supplies trout flies, cannot decide whether she is plain or beautiful:

> Mr. Spencer now regarded the young woman with some respect. She was unpretentious. Her grey eyes, rimmed with dark lashes, were wide set and tranquil and her features were agreeably irregular. She was not beautiful; she was not plain. Yes, perhaps she was beautiful. She took no pains to be beautiful. The drag of her cheap cloth coat and skirt intimated large easy curves beneath. (p. 3)

But to the young Chinese taxi-driver, Joey, "she was a lonely woman." (p. 47) To Haldar Gunnarsen she seems "strong and plain and sensible," whereas to his wife Vera she is, on first appearance, "beautiful." (p. 92) Later, when Vera has become jealous of Maggie, her view is less flattering:

> What does she wear, do, be that makes her like she is and different from me and better than me and all so quick? She wears a cotton dress, or a shirt and skirt, and so do I, or she wears blue jeans. Vera thought with a little satisfaction she shouldn't wear these jeans; she shouldn't wear slacks; she's too big; she's let her figure go. . . . (p. 148)

The one completely unambiguous and unfailing quality of Maggie, however, is her compassion. It was, as we have seen,

compassion which led her to marry Eddie Vardoe. The boy Alan
Gunnarsen sees her as bringing to the lodge "a source of fresh
happiness which flowed from her and encompassed the little
boy." (p. 121)

> Alan had come to feel that his mother had corners, but
> Mrs. Lloyd had no corners. She did not say much. Her grey
> eyes looked at him, at his very self, in kindness; she did
> not need to reproach anyone; she had a shining softness,
> even if she did not touch him. (pp. 121–22)

When the visiting fisherman, Mr. Cunningham, is caught in a
storm on the lake, it is Maggie who helps him out of his boat,
puts him to bed, and brings him a hot toddy. It is to Maggie
that Vera turns for comfort when she is soaked to the skin
after nearly drowning herself in the lake, and Maggie does not
fail her:

> Maggie, bending, drew Vera up and held her strongly and
> softly in her arms until the trembling and crying went quiet.
> She looked in front of her with troubled gaze, through the
> candlelight into the darkness and into whatever might be
> beyond the darkness. She could not think what to say to
> Vera. She did not know what words you use to exorcise
> the Evil One.
> "There then," she said with helpless compassion, patting
> Vera gently as she held her in her arms, "there then . . .
> there then . . ." (p. 202)

Looking to the future with the Gunnarsens, Maggie thinks of
herself and Alan as doing "a little more petting, a little help-
ing" (p. 210) to permit Vera to survive. And as, on the last page
of the novel, she prepares to throw the old revolver into the
lake, her last thought is of the welfare of others rather than of
herself: "Quick . . . waste no time . . . you must go back to
work . . . Angus is hungry." (p. 216)

If Maggie Vardoe is a richer and more compassionate version
of Lilly, Mrs. Severance is a more complex version of Mrs. Emblem in *Tuesday and Wednesday*. Like Mrs. Emblem, Mrs.
Severance is large, lazy, good-natured, and wise, but she has
elements of acerbity and truculence which make her a more
complicated and less predictable person. Like Maggie, she ap-

pears as a very different character at different times and from
different points of view. Her daughter Hilda tells her, half-
jokingly, that she is "a wicked old woman," (p. 30) and to Eddie
Vardoe she is "this formidable woman." (p. 54) But Mrs. Severance thinks of herself as a saviour: she says to Eddie "I am
going to bring you salvation if you want it," (p. 51) and after
she has given him the saving message, she comments, "I'm ex-
hausted, I tell you. Saving souls. Very tiring." (p. 55) Later,
however, Mrs. Severance sees herself in a far less flattering light:
"I was a *belle laide* with a funny tongue, and now I'm a plain fat
old woman with a silly tongue." (p. 79) She is, in short, a
perpetual paradox; like Walt Whitman, she is large and contains multitudes:

> The physical appearance of Mrs. Severance of heaviness
> and years was intrinsic, now, in her—was, in fact, Mrs. Sev-
> erance—and seemed to have nothing to do with age, suiting
> her perfectly as a medium for the expression of her com-
> passion for the human predicament through which she also
> had passed, for a certain contempt, and for the entertain-
> ment which she derived from her view of the human scene
> which, from the chair where she habitually sat, was both
> constricted and universal. She enjoyed her life as an observer.
> She suffered no longer from the inhibition of beauty. Passion
> was done. She was not cynical, but she was of ironical and
> amused habit. (p. 78)

Hilda accuses her of playing God by her perpetual meddling
in other people's lives, (p. 78) but Mrs. Severance thinks to
herself, "I don't really care for humanity . . . it gets between me
and my desires." (p. 97) A woman watching the fat old lady
walk down the street thinks "Isn't she peculiar?" but Mrs. Severance does not feel at all peculiar. (p. 97) Hilda's fiancé, Albert
Cousins, is attracted to Mrs. Severance because she seems so
practical: "Hilda's mother was not tender. She was matter of
fact and that suited him too. He felt increasing affection for
her," (p. 160) and there is a similar reference to her practi-
cality when Maggie wishes that "Nell Severance were here with
her acid good sense." (p. 195) When, however, she is juggling
the ancient revolver and recalling her past life on the vaudeville
stage, Nell seems the personal epitome of the romantic temperament:

"I'm stiff . . . but when I think how I used to be able to keep them moving so fluid and slow—how you had to work to get that timing! . . . and then the drums beginning, and faster and faster—all timed—and the drums louder and louder—a real drum roll . . . and I'd have the three guns going so fast they dazzled, one behind my back and one under my elegant long legs (such lovely legs!), and one out as if out towards the audience and then crack-crack-crack and the audience going crazy and me bowing and laughing like anything . . . how I loved it." (p. 77)

And at other moments in the novel, Mrs. Severance expresses a philosophy which is neither practical nor romantic but more nearly mystical:

"What do you believe?" asked Albert Cousins.
She thought for a moment, scrutinizing the end of her cigarette. "I believe in faith."
"Faith in what?" he asked.
Mrs. Severance did not answer.
"Faith in what?" he asked.
(Really, it might be Philip speaking; only he doesn't look like Philip.)
Mrs. Severance screwed up her lips, looking downwards, and so made an expression that seemed to Albert Cousins sceptical in the extreme. He waited.
"I shall not tell you today," she said, "I shall tell you another day. There is too much to say about it."
"You are cheating."
"No, I am not cheating. I believe in faith. I believe in God . . . and in man, to some extent at least." (p. 134)

"I sit on top of my little mound of years," said Mrs. Severance, "and it is natural and reasonable that I should look back, and I look back and round and I see the miraculous inter-weaving of creation . . . the everlasting web . . . and I see a stone and a word and this stub," and she threw down the stub of her cigarette, "and the man who made it, joined to the bounds of creation—has creation any bounds, Maggie? —and I see God everywhere. And Edward Vardoe (Alberto says he seems to be married or something—did you know?)

and your little Chinese boy and the other little boy and
you and me and who knows what. We are all in it together." (p. 206)

The essentially paradoxical nature of the old woman is often
suggested by the clashing adjectives which Mrs. Wilson applies
to her: she is both "disillusioned and indulgent," (p. 135) both
"worldly" and "unworldly." (p. 212)

Maggie and Mrs. Severance are the two chief and most complex characters in the novel, but the lesser characters are all
developed in the round. Eddie Vardoe, for example, is an object
of fear to Hilda Severance ("that jaunty look of his and his face
black and pasty. . . . He looks quite wicked," (p. 50) an
object of pity to her mother ("He's an unpleasant object but
worth salvation I suppose," p. 55) and a combination of the
pitiful and the fearful to Maggie:

> That night, Maggie had a dream which was a nightmare.
> . . . Out of the wood, as if it had been waiting there, walked
> a small jaunty figure, doll-like, familiar, neat in its good suit
> and hat. Edward Vardoe, incongruous in the glade, dreadful
> for her to behold, walked towards her without sign. She
> fought an impulse to turn, run, and barricade herself. Yard
> by yard he neatly came on. She stood still. He came on. Her
> heart beat to suffocation but she would not move. Edward
> Vardoe drew nearer to her, his eyes upon her, expressionless,
> walking with jaunty steps over the piney ground. She
> clenched her hands at her sides and stood strongly; as her
> heart pounded she told herself "I am not afraid. I can smile.
> Look, I am smiling!" Edward Vardoe was within six feet of
> her. She saw the familiar brownish suit, the tie, the brown
> spaniel eyes, the face which changed as she stared, to the
> face of a young anxious boy in a store, to the face of a mink
> that showed sharp teeth and ran screaming into the bushes.
> (pp. 144–45)

The roundness of Hilda Severance's character, on the other
hand, comes less from variety of point of view than from the
fact that she continuously develops as the novel proceeds. At
first she is dark, slim, introverted and unhappy, a "beautiful
cross darling" (p. 75):

Hilda went over and set her lips to her mother's face. Mrs. Severance then drew back and with the tips of her index fingers followed the wing-like lines of her daughter's dark brows. In this creamy box of her brow, the mother thought, she is nearly always unhappy—why does she hold herself so still, why can't she let down like other people, nice and easy? (pp. 75-76)

Her transformation begins when she sets out on her holiday trip:

As Mrs. Severance watched her going back to the car, she beheld her with new eyes. Not the customary Hilda coming in, but the traveller in a small clean car from—where? San Francisco perhaps? Toronto perhaps? Yes. She is very smart in that flannel suit, thought her mother. It's quite perfect. Hilda's face that could so easily storm over ("the black dog on her face," Philip used to say when she was a child) was glowing. (pp. 95-96)

Shortly after her return from this journey she falls in love with Albert Cousins, and her transformation accelerates:

Hilda moved for a short time within a luminous cloud, such a cloud as makes hard-headed people soft-headed. She had never before given herself up to love; because she was self-protecting, mistrustful of herself and of others, she had not dared to commit herself to love. . . . I am too old, Hilda thought, to be so happy; but how happy I am. (p. 156)

As Albert sees her, "Hilda's coolness had melted to a tenderness that surprised him and endeared her." (p. 160) By the end of the novel Hilda is a mother, and her transformation is complete:

"Baby is such a darling and so good. You should see him. We call him Monty after Montgomery, Rufus' mother's maiden name. I will send you a photograph. Now that we have changed his formula . . ." and so on.

Can this be Hilda Severance, the scornful one, daughter of Nell Severance? No, this is Hilda Cousins, blender of bottles, mother of Monty, who is writing. (p. 212)

Hilda Severance, it is clear, has been redeemed by love; Vera Gunnarsen, a somewhat similar woman, is almost destroyed by jealousy. Married to a good, if crippled, husband, and mother of a fine son, Alan, she is not satisfied: "Her heart and her head told her that she should be satisfied; yet she was not." (p. 85) Her jealousy is first directed against Three Loon Lake, for which her husband has so strong a love: she "developed a jealousy against the lake as against a person." (p. 87) Then her jealousy transfers itself to the efficient and apparently happy Maggie:

> When the little sliver of jealousy ran into her flesh, she did not pull it out. Her flesh festered pleasantly round the sliver. She indulged in the pleasure of the pain of her small growing jealousy. Since jealousy is a luxury which soon becomes a necessity to those who have felt its sharp enthralling pain, Vera became unhappy again. She had for some time, now, been that poor Vera Gunnarsen, and habit is strong. There was easy harmony between her husband and Maggie Lloyd. She looked for something more, and there was nothing more. Alan was fonder of Mrs. Lloyd than Vera liked. Maggie had succeeded everywhere where she, Vera, seemed to have failed. Maggie seemed unaware of it. All this was not easy to bear. (p. 110)

She alternates between jealousy of others and pity of herself:

> The sight of Maggie, happy and beloved, passed and repassed before her mind. Vera in her frequent moods of self-pity said to herself I never had a break, did I, my mother never loved me . . . and now . . . look! no, I never had a break. She carried her childhood on her back, and could not—or would not—set it down. Jealousy, how potent it is, the very agent of destruction, a seed that grows. No, a poison that spreads and infests every part. No, the worm that consumes and never consumes. How shall a mind be purged? (pp. 148–49)

When her jealousy drives her to the very brink of suicide, she is saved, and precariously at that, only by Maggie's self-sacrificial love. Mrs. Severance thinks of her as "the unhappy Vera; housebound without an opening window; hell-bound, I think," (p. 209) and Vera thinks of herself as lost ("Oh, what can I do? Something has changed in me and I am lost" p. 210). Only the prac-

tical, compassionate, never-despairing Maggie holds out any
hope:

> "I think," said Maggie at last, "f'rinstance, Alan and I can
> do a little more petting, a little helping. And, Henry—you
> and Haldar too . . ."
>
> "Gosh . . . me? . . ." exclaimed Henry Corder in alarm.
> "I couldn't pet anybody—never done such a thing in all my
> life!"
>
> "I'll teach you, Henry," laughed Maggie. Haldar did not
> laugh. In his mind was the dark lamentable knowledge that
> some years ago something had slipped, just a little, at first.
> Perhaps it was Vera's fault. Perhaps it was his own fault.
> Perhaps it was that damn hip. By this time he stood alone
> and he did not know where Vera stood; if she were another
> woman, and not his wife, he would not care where she stood.
>
> He left Henry and Maggie talking beside the gate and
> limped back to the house. Alan came running home in the
> dusk.
>
> "Come, son," said Haldar. "Let's go in and see how your
> mother's getting along."
>
> "Sure," said Alan, breathless.
>
> Henry Corder turned and looked back at them.
>
> "Can you work it somehow, Maggie, so's them two gits
> together again?" he said.
>
> "I can't, Henry. Maybe Alan can without ever knowing it.
> Perhaps there's a way. I think there might be a way. It isn't
> easy and it's not going to be easy."
>
> "I'll tell the cockeyed world," said Henry Corder. He medi-
> tated, spitting—from time to time—into the night.
>
> Then "It's cold," he said, and they went in. (pp. 210–11)

That scene, in which so much more is hinted at than is said,
suggests the subtlety with which this novel is written. By the
repetition of certain simple motifs, Mrs. Wilson gives to them a
symbolic significance far beyond their normal desert. In the total
context of the novel, Maggie's seemingly ordinary statement, "I
think there might be a way," has a greatly enlarged significance,
as does Henry Corder's act of spitting into the night. We are
brought, in other words, to a discussion of the theme of the novel.

III   *Thematic Patterns*

Maggie's statement takes on such force because the whole novel is concerned with the opposition between movement and stasis. Movement is life, stasis is death; those characters who "have no corners," such as Maggie, who "swim," have "generous easy curves," who persist in believing that there is a way, are the survivors, the victors, the affirmers of life; those such as Vera, who have corners, who carry their childhood on their backs, (p. 148) who try to hold on too tightly, (p. 149) are the victims, the deniers of life. Life is a continuous cycle of movement, a rhythmic round:

> The picket fence and the crosses would be covered by snow in the winter. Then the spring sunshine beating on the hillside would melt the snow, and the snow would run off, and the crosses would stand revealed again. And in the spring the Canada geese would pass in their arrows of flight, honking, honking, high over the silent hillside. Later in the season, when the big white moon was full, coyotes would sing among the hills at night, on and on in the moonlight, stopping, and then all beginning again together. Spring flowers would come—a few—in the coarse grass. Then, in the heat of the summer, bright small snakes and beetles would slip through the grasses, and the crickets would dryly sing. Then the sumac would turn scarlet, and the skeins of wild geese would return in their swift pointed arrows of flight to the south, passing high overhead between the great hills. Their musical cry would drop down into the valley lying in silence. Then would come the snow, and the three wooden crosses would be covered again. (pp. 65–66)

Subtly, but in a multitude of ways, this sense of the cosmic rhythm is communicated throughout the novel. Images of rhythmic movement—of flight, flow, swimming, weaving—occur and recur on almost every page. The novel opens with the return of migrating birds—"Ten twenty fifty brown birds flew past the window and then a few stragglers, out of sight"—and concludes with a picture of swimming fish:

> When all was still the fish, who had fled, returned, flickering, weaving curiously over the Swamp Angel. Then flickering, weaving, they resumed their way. (p. 216)

Even mountains are "fluid, not solid," (p. 1) and the city of Vancouver, expanding its suburbs, "is crawling on." (p. 12) Time, of course, flows:

> These actions [making dinner], which were familiar and almost mechanical, took on, tonight, the significance of movement forward, of time felt in the act of passing, of a moment being reached (time always passes, but it is in the nature of things that we seldom observe it flowing, flying, past). (p. 6)

Time flows, but there is another kind of time that jerks and grinds against the natural temporal rhythm:

> Joey did not yet know Time that flowed smoothly, as in this place. In all of his life Time had jerked by with a rat-tat-tat, with the beating of a clock, with shrill cries to come to supper, with the starting up of an engine, with the slamming of doors, with the change of radio programme, with the traffic, with voices. . . . (p. 142)

The air continuously flows:

> An expanse of air in the night, endless, soft, fluent, still, blowing, moving, cleaving, closing, sliding through dark leaves and branches and past houses and lamp-posts and black silent areas and bright areas of sound, movement and smell, separating lover from lover, victim from approaching thief, thief from hunter, mother from child, quite hid Maggie afar from Edward Vardoe who walked with prim quick steps along the shabby sidewalk in the dark on Capitol Hill. (p. 25)

And in this moving air trees shift rhythmically against the sky:

> As she lay in the dark in the hard double bed and smelt the sweet rough-dried sheets, she saw through the cabin windows the tops of tall firs moving slowly in a small arc, and back, against the starred sky. Slowly they moved, obliterating stars, and then revealing them. (p. 31)

Rivers flow—the Fraser dangerously and silently, the Illecillewat dancing and silvery (p. 61)—clouds drift across the blue, (p. 37) and the sun passes over the arc of sky between the mountains. (p. 38) Spring pours in "over the whole countryside" (p. 40) and the very earth seems to flow: "the road passed between grassy mounds, rippling, flowing, it seemed, out of each other." (p. 64) Canada geese "pass in their arrows of flight, honking, high over the silent hillside." (p. 65) Trees "marched in thin armies up the runnels of the hills." (p. 71) The osprey flies, then dives to seize the leaping trout. (pp. 83–84)

The relationship of human beings to these cosmic rhythms is twofold: they are at once spectators of them and participants in them.

From the contemplation of them they can obtain either a sense of universal harmony or a sense of their own insignificance. Mrs. Wilson suggests that both these responses are legitimate, although she seems to imply—and says explicitly through Mrs. Severance—that the effect of harmony is and should be dominant. For Maggie, the effect is almost always affirmative:

> The west wind blew down the river channel; and the wind, the river, and the quiet sound of the rippling river, a sigh in the pine trees surrounded by stillness, and the stars in the arc of the night sky between the mountains, the scent of the pines, the ancient rocks below and above her, and the pine-made earth, a physical languor, her solitude, her troubled mind, and a lifting of her spirit to God by the river brought tears to her eyes. I am on a margin of life, she thought, and she remembered that twice before in her own life she had known herself to be taken to that margin of a world which was powerful and close. (p. 40)

> One night she saw, north of the lake, a pale glow invade the sky. Maggie got up and pulled a blanket round her. The pale glow was greenish, no, a hot colour rose up and quickly took possession. The colour changed. The vast sky moved as with banners. The sky was an intimation of something still vaster, and spiritual. For two hours Maggie watched enraptured the great folding, playing, flapping of these draperies of light in heaven, transient, unrepeated, sliding up and down the sky. After declaiming lavishly, the great

> Northern Lights faded with indifference as one who is bored
> and—deploring display—says I may come back but only if
> I choose; I do as I wish; I am powerful; I am gone but I am
> here. The orthodox stars, which had been washed away,
> returned palely. Night was resumed, and Maggie slept. (pp.
> 124–25)

For Vera, on the other hand, the effect of the movement of nature
is one of immense hostility:

> The faint light that remained in the western sky did not
> penetrate the wood. Vera sought the path that lay on the
> right side of the lake. Trees met overhead, and branches,
> crossing the unfrequented path, struck at her. All was so
> dark under the trees that she could not see her way but
> had to find it with feet that felt and with hands that flinched
> against the branches. She whimpered as she went because
> the whimpering seemed to bear her company in the immense
> hostility of her world. (p. 198)

But it is Mrs. Severance who makes most explicit the novel's
affirmative theme of universal harmony, when she declares that
from the "top of [her] little mound of years" she sees "the
miraculous interweaving of creation . . . the everlasting web."
(p. 206)

But man is not only a spectator of the cosmic rhythm; he is
also a participant in it. Time and time again in the novel analogies
are drawn between man and his natural environment, animate
and inanimate. Rivers flow, and so does traffic; Eddie Vardoe is
described as "swimming in a murky sea of emotions" (p. 26);
groups of immigrants "surge from the United States and from
Vancouver Island" (p. 33); just as the sun passes over the arc
of sky, so does "a plane, full of invisible beings, roar across the
patch of sky between the mountains" (p. 38); human speech
flows "up and down the stairs" (p. 45); power flows from Mrs.
Severance (p. 75) as elsewhere it flows from the mighty Fraser
River; human dreams flow from "some subterranean course" (p.
145); the human blood is a flowing tide ("Colour flowed over
Maggie's face and stained her neck" p. 189); human beings are
as subject as nature to sudden storms ("He [Haldar] began to
be swept by a private tornado which, at one touch of his wife's

hand, would have torn him apart, raged round the room, and destroyed them both." p. 197)

Maggie Lloyd, above all, feels her kinship with the natural world. She watches an osprey catch a fish, and then have its prey stolen by the still stronger eagle, and she ponders:

> Did a bird's rage or a bird's acceptance possess him? There was nothing he could do. The eagle disappeared into the blue which at the horizon was veil-like, mist-like, carrying the fish, pontoon-wise. Maggie returned to her reality. She had been lifted by this battle of birds with its defeat and its victory. She took the oars and rowed slowly down the lake. Fish rose, and fell, splashing, far and near, and the loon, swimming almost beside her, uttered cries.
>
> As she returned to the shore and reality, Maggie felt like a swimmer who will dive in, and will swim strongly, this way, that way, straight ahead, as he shall choose. But he will swim. (pp. 115–16)

>   .   .   .   .
> Her avatar tells her that she is one with her brothers the seal and the porpoise who tumble in the salt waves; and as she splashes and cleaves through the fresh water she is one with them. But her avatar had better warn her that she is not really seal or porpoise—that is just a sortie into the past, made by the miracle of water—and in a few minutes she will be brought to earth, brought again to walk the earth where she lives and must stay. Who would not be a seal or a porpoise? They have a nice life, lived in the cool water with fun and passion, without human relations, Courtesy Week, or a flame thrower. (p. 129)

Maggie's salvation is that she "rolls with the punches," moves in harmony with the cosmic rhythms. The unsympathetic characters in the book, chiefly Eddie Vardoe and Vera Gunnarsen, maintain a mechanical, unnatural rhythm (rather like the unnatural time that Joey became accustomed to in the city of Vancouver) or attempt to hold back the movement of time. Eddie is described as a "poor human doll, running from room to room in the empty house" (pp. 24–25) and as "a small jaunty figure, doll-like . . . incongruous in the glade," (p. 145) and we picture him walking with the stiff mechanical stride of a clock-work doll. Vera, on the other hand, tries to hold back time: "she carried her childhood on her back, and could not—or would not—set it down," (p. 148) and she tries to hold her husband and son too tightly even though she knows that by so doing she is apt to lose them. (p. 149) Her alienation from nature and the rhythmic movement of nature is expressed in Mrs. Severance's final compassionate comment upon her: "The unhappy Vera; housebound without an opening window; hell-bound, I think." (p. 209)

IV   *The Controlling Symbol*

This opposition between movement and stasis is also conveyed by the symbolic use of the ancient revolver, the Swamp Angel. The revolver is a many-faceted symbol, but its chief meaning seems to be that in treasuring it Mrs. Severance is attempting to hold the substance of her own romantic past, whereas in surrendering it she is freely accepting change, the forward rhythm of life, and her own approaching death as a natural part of the cosmic cycle.

Our first glimpse of the Swamp Angel comes in the epigraph, where we read:

"Swamp Angel. An 8-inch, 200-pound . . . gun, mounted in a swamp by the Federals, at the siege (1863) of Charleston, S.C." *Webster's Dictionary.*

Subsequently, there was an issue of small revolvers, inscribed "Swamp Angel." (p. V)

Here it seems to stand for the past, for violence, and possibly for courage. The particular revolver which Mrs. Severance owns is introduced as "the family pet" used by both Mrs. Severance and her father in their juggling acts. (p. 28–29) At intervals throughout the first half of the novel we see Mrs. Severance toying with the small gun, and to her it is always a source of pleasure and comfort. To Hilda, on the other hand, it is a source of irritation, since it reminds her of her unhappy childhood and of the way in which she was teased by her schoolmates for having a juggler as a mother. Hilda had never told her mother of the displeasure this gun caused her, and so it "had been suffered to remain as the symbol of years of life gone away." (p. 58) When Mrs. Severance decides that she must get rid of the gun, she reflects: "The

Angel must go . . . because it is a symbol and too dear." (p. 99)
She speaks of giving it up in words which recall Christ's saying
"He that shall lose his life for my sake shall save it"—she says
"I shall lose it and save it." (p. 101) Thus it is really her past
life that she is surrendering: she is giving herself up to the
future. As she sees her housekeeper take away the box in which
she has carefully packed the gun for shipment to Maggie, she
ponders:

> She did not look at the shoe-box as Mrs. Spink went with
> sprightly step out of the room, taking the box and the letter.
> After all, the box contained her life and she could not look.
> Her endeared symbol was gone and she would not touch it
> any more. I have nothing now but the reality, she thought
> stoically and fairly cheerfully, and at this moment it doesn't
> seem much. I am really too old in living. She recognized
> for a bright revealing instant that came, and then passed,
> that life and the evening were closing in. Very well. (p. 105)

Incidentally, it seems probable that Mrs. Severance's name is
meant to convey her readiness to sever herself from her past:
Mrs. Wilson often uses the Dickensian device of the suggestive
name, as exemplified by Mrs. Emblem, Mort and Myrt in *Tuesday
and Wednesday* and Topaz in *The Innocent Traveller*.

It is significant that it is Maggie to whom the revolver is sent,
and that it is she who, on the last page of the novel, throws it
into the lake. Maggie, as we have seen, stands for the individual
who looks resolutely to the future, and who is ready to rely upon
her own resources. Romanticism, in a sense, has paid its tribute
to realism. Maggie approves of Mrs. Severance's action in surrendering the gun:

> About the Angel. It may not be very significant to you,
> sending it away, but it is to me. It was right to do that. . . .
> I am so sure that our ability to throw away the substance,
> to lose all yet keep the essence, is very important. (p. 175)

But before she carries out Mrs. Severance's orders to throw the
gun into the lake, she reflects on its value:

> . . . This revolver is far too good to be thrown away.
>   The Swamp Angel in its empty years or so has caused
> death and astonishment and jealousy and affection and one

night it frightened Edward Vardoe on Maggie's behalf,
although Maggie does not know that, and soon it will be
gone. It will be a memory, and then not even a memory,
for there will be no one to remember it. Yet does the essence
of all custom and virtue perish? How can she know? Quick
. . . waste no time . . . you must go back to work . . . Angus
is hungry . . . throw that little gun into the lake at once. (pp.
215–16)

Maggie's practical realism triumphs, and she throws the gun. The
fish who weave their way over it obviously symbolize the forces
of the present and future, which must take precedence over the
inert past.

V   Subsidiary Image-Patterns

Although this central theme of the importance of cosmic rhythm
and movement is carried mainly by the pervasive images of motion and the thematic motif of the Swamp Angel, there are
subsidiary patterns of imagery which reinforce it. The chief
subsidiary image pattern contrasts organic life with the inorganic:
generally speaking the organic is symbolic of movement and
vitality, the inorganic of stasis or death. Maggie, for example,
is compared to a "bird who obstinately builds again its destroyed
nest," (p. 2) whereas Eddie's life is said to be "broken off, splin-
tered like a stick." (p. 29) Eddie is described by Mrs. Severance
as "putty in the hand," (p. 55) and Vera's jealousy is "a little
sliver." (p. 110) Self-pity is compared to dynamite, (p. 53) Hilda
feels "the needle of compunction," (p. 80) work is a "tight wire,"
(p. 139) jealousy is said to be not a seed that grows but a poison
that spreads. (p. 148)

Occasionally, however, there is recognition of the evil and
violence lurking in the organic world. When Maggie is struck
by remorse for having left her husband "a thought as thin and
cruel as a pipe fish cut through her mind." (p. 38) When she has
her nightmare vision of Eddie, she sees him as "a mink that
showed sharp teeth." (p. 145) Vera's jealousy is not only a sliver
and a poison, it is also a worm that consumes. (pp. 148–49) A letter offering Maggie another job is to Haldar Gunnarsen "as ac-
ceptable as a rattlesnake." (p. 189) This suggests the essential

ambiguity of the natural world: it is rhythmic and persistent, but it can also be violent and destructive. The double vision is perhaps best expressed by the two climactic episodes in the novel which involve the animal kingdom: the scene between the osprey and the eagle, (p. 115) and the scene between the fawn and the kitten. (pp. 125–27). The former scene is the vision of experience: the world as a battleground of contending appetites; the latter is the vision of innocence: the world as a playground of mutual curiosity and respect. The interesting thing is that Maggie finds both spectacles heartening, presumably because in her practical, affirmative realism (which is another way of describing what Mrs. Wilson might have called her innocence) she sees both the battle and the play as necessary parts of the universal cycle.

Another image pattern whereby Mrs. Wilson conveys her sense of the ambiguity of the relationship between man and his world is that of light and darkness. The chief effect of the recurrent imagery of this sort is to suggest the mysteriousness of the extra-human world. Light is almost always associated with the human world of rooms, houses, streets, and automobiles, whereas darkness is associated either with the unknown or the hostile. By the frequent repetition of these allusions to light and darkness, a simple sentence such as "Beyond lay the dark garden and the invisible woodshed" (p. 23) takes on a definitely uncanny effect. Perhaps the most vivid examples of this use of the contrast of light and darkness occur at the time of Vera's near-suicide: as she makes her way to the lake the darkness of the woods suggests to her overwrought imagination "the immense hostility of the world," (p. 198) and when Maggie takes her in and comforts her there are several allusions to the light of the candle which Maggie is holding, and the statement "a room lit by a candle and in a silent and solitary place is a world within itself." (p. 201)

This emphasis upon the mysteriousness and potential violence of the extra-human universe is complemented by a recognition of human vulnerability. Mrs. Severance warns Eddie that he will "go down, and out of sight," (p. 54) and she reflects that her daughter Hilda "being only a human being, would never in life be truly safe." (p. 105) When the visiting fisherman is caught out in the storm on the lake, the author comments, "It is a terrible thing to be alone, weak, and in a storm, far from the

indifferent shore." (p. 183) Mrs. Severance asserts that "we have
no immunity and we may as well realize it," (p. 207) and as we
have seen there are moments when even the resolute Maggie
feels that she is defeated and can swim no more.

It is this sense of human vulnerability which leads Mrs. Wilson
to stress so often in the novel the role of compassion. As Mrs.
Severance puts it, "we are all in it together," (p. 206) and she
quotes Donne to the effect that "No man is an Iland, I am involved in mankind." (p. 207) The word compassion occurs many
times in the novel, and there are several important scenes which
display its operation.

Another consequence of the recognition of human vulnerability
is the stress placed on various forms of human relationship. The
importance of a proper relationship between parents and children
is brought out in the account given of Hilda's childhood un-
happiness, of the Chinese family's closeness and mutual de-
pendence, of Alan Gunnarsen's relations with his mother and
father, of Hilda's love for her baby, of Maggie's grief for her
lost child. The marriage relationship is also explored from many
points of view and in many forms: there is the unhappy marriage
between Maggie and Eddie, the common-law but extremely
affectionate marriage between Mrs. Severance and her husband,
the strained and fragile tie between Vera and Haldar Gunnarsen,
the apparently ideal relationship between Hilda Severance and
Albert Cousins. In an unhappy marriage, the partners may become, as Maggie and Eddie did, "each other's executioners." (p.
39) But in a happy marriage there is "a hidden sweetness . . .
which reveals itself between two people in the common ways
of touch and sight and peculiar word." (p. 89)

We have now seen something of the complexity of theme in
this novel. It is not just a matter of man recognizing his part
in the cosmic cycle and thus automatically finding fulfillment:
the cosmos is mysterious and violent, and even at his most
resolute man needs the compassion of his fellows and the consolation of his family. Whether the cosmos itself is ultimately
benevolent, indifferent, or malevolent is never finally answered,
although I think that we are meant to accept the God-affirming
benevolent views of Mrs. Severance and Maggie rather than the
malevolent view of Vera. But at any rate the novel is no expression of easy optimism: man is a swimmer in a dark lake

which may at any moment break into storm, and he is a creature uneasily poised in his nature between the animality of the seal and the divinity of God:

> Her avatar tells her that she is one with her brothers the seal and the porpoise who tumble and tumble in the salt waves; and as she splashes and cleaves through the fresh water she is one with them. . . .
> The water, that element that bears her up and impedes her and cleaves and flies away and falls as only water can, transforms her, because she can swim. If she could not swim, ah . . . then . . . it would no doubt kill her and think nothing of it. But, since she can swim, she swims strongly out into the lake, forgetting past and future, thrusting the pleasant water with arms and legs, and then, quite suddenly, she turns on her back and floats. She is contented. She is not a seal. She is a god floating there with the sun beating down on her face with fatal beneficent warmth, and the air is good. . . .
> The god and the seal are out there in the water. Or perhaps they are not there unless the swimmer is there too. (pp. 129–30)

VI *Final Unity*

The thematic implications of *Swamp Angel* are so fascinating that they tend to distract our attention from other aspects of the novel. It is a fully integrated work of art. Structurally, it begins with the flying of birds and ends with the swimming of fishes; its action takes place exactly in one year, from early spring to early spring; it begins and ends with Maggie Lloyd throwing something away—a marriage that has gone dead, and a revolver which symbolizes the dead past. Although it employs the technique of the multiple point of view, the lives and attitudes of all the characters intersect to the extent that we have the sense of a single web being continuously woven. Three dominant patterns of imagery—movement and stasis, organic and inorganic life, light and dark—interweave to reinforce this sense of unity. The unity is further enhanced by the employment of thematic motifs, of which the Swamp Angel is the chief example and

Maggie's treasured yellow Chinese bowl a second conspicuous one. The novel is punctuated by vivid passages describing Vancouver and other parts of British Columbia, the encounters of birds, animals, and fishes, and such human activities as fishing and manual labour, but none of these passages are unrelated to the theme, or have at all the air of interpolated set-pieces. Everything weaves together into a web of great, if sometimes terrible, beauty.

Love and Salt Water (1956)

L OVE and Salt Water[1] is the last and probably the least re-
warding of Mrs. Wilson's novels. That is not to say that it is
a bad novel: it is subtle and sensitive, and embodies most of its
author's special skills and insights. But it has not quite the near-
perfection displayed by The Innocent Traveller, the two novellas
in The Equations of Love, and Swamp Angel.

I Characterization

The characters in Love and Salt Water bear strong family re-
semblances to those in other of Mrs. Wilson's novels, but they
are less striking. The part of the wise old woman, so effectively
carried in Tuesday and Wednesday by Mrs. Emblem and in
Swamp Angel by Mrs. Severance, is here assigned to Aunt Maury
Peake, but we never feel her reality as strongly. She is the one
to whom Ellen turns for help when her mother dies, and who
comforts Ellen and Johnny when they are nearly drowned in
the climactic episode of the book. She is described as one who
"blesses everything she touches" (p. 169) and as being "like God
from Heaven." (p. 178) But she shares this role of the comforter
with Susan Cuppy, never utters any speeches as memorable as
those of Mrs. Emblem and Mrs. Severance, and is altogether less
subtly and complexly portrayed. The role of the lonely spinster,
played by Victoria May Tritt in Tuesday and Wednesday, is
assigned in this novel to the much less memorable Maud Sneddon.
The neurotic, overly possessive wife, embodied in Swamp Angel

in Vera Gunnarsen, is here much less strikingly represented by Ellen's sister, Nora Cuppy.

The relative decline in strength of characterization, however, is most clearly seen in the central character. Ellen Cuppy is cast in the same mould as Lilly and Maggie—she is self-reliant, a strong swimmer like Maggie in both the literal and metaphorical senses, adaptable, courageous, decisive, slightly ruthless on occasion and yet fundamentally tender and protective in her relations with other people. She moves us far less deeply than Lilly and Maggie, however, perhaps because she is of a higher class and because the adverse circumstances against which she must contend are so much less forbidding. Unlike Lilly, who had to fight her way up to respectability from the depths of degradation, Ellen is born into a prosperous Vancouver family, goes to a private school, serves in the Wrens during the War, becomes private secretary to a wealthy Saskatoon investor, and spends her spare time playing tennis and badminton. The difficulties which beset her—the sudden death of her mother, the re-marriage of her father, a broken love affair with Huw Peake, getting badly scarred on the face while attempting to rescue her young nephew from drowning—are conveyed to us with Mrs. Wilson's customary skill, but it is only in the last of the series that we feel our sympathies deeply engaged. The scene in which Ellen, who has taken a seven-year-old boy out in a rowboat in order that he may realize his dream of seeing a seal, succeeds in rescuing the boy when the rowboat is capsized by the swell of a passing Vancouver ferry is a truly powerful one, so powerful that it almost redeems the novel from the charges we have been bringing against it.

II Structure

But the very fact that this scene stands out so vividly indicates a further weakness of the novel: it is a relatively loose series of scenes, rather than a fully integrated work of art as was *Swamp Angel.* Mrs. Wilson seeks in various ways to bind the parts of the novel together, but the binding never fully takes. Part I, dealing with Ellen's childhood, the death of her mother, and a long sea voyage which she takes with her bereaved father, culminates in a storm in which a sailor-boy is drowned; in order

to connect this with the near-drowning of Ellen's nephew, the
climax of Part III and indeed of the whole novel, there is an
echo of the earlier drowning in the phrase used by the sailor-boy,
"I sea-boy." (pp. 35, 176) Ellen's thought in Part I, that if she
tells nobody about her mother's death it will not be real (p. 16)
is echoed in Nora's similar thought about Johnny's deafness in
Part III. (p. 146) The novel begins on the eve of Nora's wedding,
and ends on the eve of Ellen's. At the beginning of the novel
Ellen is convinced that Morgan Peake is not a fit husband for
her sister; at the end, Ellen chooses Morgan to accompany her
to the station to meet her own fiancé because in the intervening
decade she has come to recognize Morgan's worth. Such devices
do something to bind the parts of the novel together, but they
fall well short of the effectiveness of such thematic motifs in
Swamp Angel as the revolver itself and the migrating birds and
swimming fish.

It is really Part II of the novel which defeats Mrs. Wilson's
attempts to make this story a fully integrated one. She seems to
have been conscious of this difficulty herself, for at the end of
Part I she puts this passage, which seems to be an *apologia* for
the inadequacy of Part II:

In her much later life the long period which elapsed between the voyage and the meeting with her husband at the
railway station seemed—erroneously—to Ellen to have passed
with the fluidity and the sometimes violence of dreams, and
therefore to be of no true significance. It is a fact that to
one person a voyage may mean only a departure and an
arrival, an expense incurred, only a happy lapse of coloured
time, only an embarking and a disembarking— the distance
between two places on a map which may be pink or even
blue; but to Ellen the voyage was a shaking and transforming
experience with which nothing in her future personal life
was comparable, not even the events of the war because she
was only one of millions of participants, and certainly not
the years during which she worked for old Mr. Platt in
Saskatoon—until she met George on the railway platform,
and for the duration of her life thereafter. There is a curious
semblance of reality in those of our years which are certainly valid, but seem to slide, and differ from our years of

reality. During those years of elision we live, of course, with relative intensity, and those years mark, retard, hasten, improve, or worsen us, and, alas, may affect some of those with whom we come into touch to a degree of pleasure, exasperation or even of damage, of which we are only partly aware; but then the true years of our life arrive—or do not arrive—and we forget those other irrelevant years which may, since Time is an agent, some day stir, and take their unexpected vengeance in a variety of ingenious ways. Such, at least, was Ellen's experience. (pp. 60-61)

There is a certain lameness about that passage, and its involved style reflects an inner uncertainty on its author's part. The thought is muddled, and the reference to Time taking its vengeance is a puzzling one which nothing in the remainder of the novel, so far as I can see, succeeds in clarifying. At the very least, this passage is an artistic blunder, since it tells us in advance that nothing of significance comparable to the voyage is to happen to Ellen until the meeting with George, which occurs on the very last pages of the novel. The whole of Part II, and much of Part III, have thus been dismissed in advance.

I suspect that passage of being a belated—and in my view misguided—interpolation. There are other hints that this novel was several times reworked by its author in an attempt to remedy its deficiencies. The opening pages of Part III, for example, by giving the full names of Ellen and Nora and by recapitulating other information already known to readers of Parts I and II, suggest that at one time this was intended as the beginning of an independent *novella*. And the sudden intrusion and quick disappearance of Merri Thompson on pages 152-53, and the reference to a "last time," suggest that there was at one time a scene introducing Merri which was subsequently deleted.

These, however, are relatively minor matters. The chief ways in which *Love and Salt Water* falls short of its predecessors are its thematic uncertainty and its relative paucity of unifying images and symbols.

III   *The Major Theme*

I believe that there is a single over-riding theme in *Love and Salt Water*, but it is far less clearly articulated than are the themes in Vera Gunnarsen, is here much less strikingly represented by Ellen's sister, Nora Cuppy.

The relative decline in strength of characterization, however, is most clearly seen in the central character. Ellen Cuppy is cast in the same mould as Lilly and Maggie—she is self-reliant, a strong swimmer like Maggie in both the literal and metaphorical senses, adaptable, courageous, decisive, slightly ruthless on occasion and yet fundamentally tender and protective in her relations with other people. She moves us far less deeply than Lilly and Maggie, however, perhaps because she is of a higher class and because the adverse circumstances against which she must contend are so much less forbidding. Unlike Lilly, who had to fight her way up to respectability from the depths of degradation, Ellen is born into a prosperous Vancouver family, goes to a private school, serves in the Wrens during the War, becomes private secretary to a wealthy Saskatoon investor, and spends her spare time playing tennis and badminton. The difficulties which beset her—the sudden death of her mother, the re-marriage of her father, a broken love affair with Huw Peake, getting badly scarred on the face while attempting to rescue her young nephew from drowning—are conveyed to us with Mrs. Wilson's customary skill, but it is only in the last of the series that we feel our sympathies deeply engaged. The scene in which Ellen, who has taken a seven-year-old boy out in a rowboat in order that he may realize his dream of seeing a seal, succeeds in rescuing the boy when the rowboat is capsized by the swell of a passing Vancouver ferry is a truly powerful one, so powerful that it almost redeems the novel from the charges we have been bringing against it.

II *Structure*

But the very fact that this scene stands out so vividly indicates a further weakness of the novel: it is a relatively loose series of scenes, rather than a fully integrated work of art as was *Swamp Angel.* Mrs. Wilson seeks in various ways to bind the parts of the novel together, but the binding never fully takes. Part I, dealing with Ellen's childhood, the death of her mother, and a long sea voyage which she takes with her bereaved father, culminates in a storm in which a sailor-boy is drowned; in order

Love and Salt Water (1956)

L OVE and Salt Water[1] is the last and probably the least re-warding of Mrs. Wilson's novels. That is not to say that it is a bad novel: it is subtle and sensitive, and embodies most of its author's special skills and insights. But it has not quite the near-perfection displayed by *The Innocent Traveller*, the two novellas in *The Equations of Love*, and *Swamp Angel*.

I · Characterization

The characters in *Love and Salt Water* bear strong family re-semblances to those in other of Mrs. Wilson's novels, but they are less striking. The part of the wise old woman, so effectively carried in *Tuesday and Wednesday* by Mrs. Emblem and in *Swamp Angel* by Mrs. Severance, is here assigned to Aunt Maury Peake, but we never feel her reality as strongly. She is the one to whom Ellen turns for help when her mother dies, and who comforts Ellen and Johnny when they are nearly drowned in the climactic episode of the book. She is described as one who "blesses everything she touches" (p. 169) and as being "like God from Heaven." (p. 178) But she shares this role of the comforter with Susan Cuppy, never utters any speeches as memorable as those of Mrs. Emblem and Mrs. Severance, and is altogether less subtly and complexly portrayed. The role of the lonely spinster, played by Victoria May Tritt in *Tuesday and Wednesday*, is assigned in this novel to the much less memorable Maud Sneddon. The neurotic, overly possessive wife, embodied in *Swamp Angel*

of *Swamp Angel* and *Lilly's Story*. The theme is suggested by the title: this is a novel about love and loneliness, union and estrangement. Since Mrs. Wilson's family had known Matthew Arnold (as we learn from *The Innocent Traveller*), it seems certain that she knew his poem "To Marguerite," and it seems to me that it is the thought of that poem which lies behind much of *Love and Salt Water:*

> Yes: in the sea of life enisled,
>   With echoing straits between us thrown.
> Dotting the shoreless watery wild,
>   We mortal millions live *alone*.
> The islands feel the enclasping flow,
> And then their endless bounds they know.
>
> But when the moon their hollows lights,
>   And they are swept by balms of spring,
> And in their glens, on starry nights,
>   The nightingales divinely sing;
> And lovely notes, from shore to shore,
> Across the sounds and channels pour;
>
> O then a longing like despair
>   Is to their farthest caverns sent!
> For surely once, they feel, we were
>   Parts of a single continent.
> Now round us spreads the watery plain—
> O might our marges meet again!
>
> Who ordered that their longing's fire
>   Should be, as soon as kindled, cooled?
> Who renders vain their deep desire?—
>   A god, a god their severance ruled;
> And bade betwixt their shores to be
> The unplumbed, salt, estranging sea.

The essential loneliness of human beings, and their more or less successful attempts to overcome this loneliness by love, form the basic stuff of this novel. Mr. Cuppy is lonely for his wife Susan, and attempts to overcome this loneliness by his love for, and second marriage to, Nicola Gracey. Ellen feels "very much alone on this sea, and yet very much together with all the other people who were also alone." (p. 46) She grows "almost fond" of the

miserly old Mr. Platt because "he was so solitary." (p. 89) But
Platt has largely conquered his loneliness by his intense love of
money—he was "a lonely old man who was not in the least lonely."
(p. 100) Witnessing the loneliness of Miss Maud Sneddon, Ellen
fears that she too some day may be a lonely old woman. (pp. 123-
24) The mongoloid elder son of Nora and Morgan Peake is
lonely—a "little cipher sitting in seclusion" (p. 144)—and Morgan
tries to mitigate his loneliness with paternal love.

The love which seeks to master loneliness has many equations.
There are as many varieties of love in this novel as in *Lilly's Story*
or *Swamp Angel*. The marital love between Nora and Morgan
seems very unromantic to Ellen, but it suffices Nora: "She was
reasonably fond of him, and, as she did not know the force of
passion, she retained her unflawed good looks, and the train of
her life in which she sat as a beautiful passenger was drawn as
it were by a diesel engine which made travelling too smooth."
(p. 8) Nora's lack of ardour suits Morgan, for he is not ardent
himself—love for him is basically a wish "to console, to support
her." (p. 184) Their marriage is one of two solitudes who, in
Rilke's words, "protect, and touch, and greet each other:" we
several times see them going to bed in their separate rooms, but
they call out "good night" from one room to the other (see, for
example, p. 192).

There are other varieties of marital love in the novel. That
between Frank and Susan Cuppy is strong and sure—but it does
not prevent Frank from thinking his own thoughts even when
Susan is talking to him. (p. 12) It is because his love for his first
wife was so strong that Frank falls in love with Nicola—a development we watch in detailed stages in the latter half of Part I. The
second marriage rather shocks Ellen, but in her sensible way she
comes to recognize its validity:

> His wife Nicola, grown heavier, suited him well. Ellen felt
> affection for Nicola, but it seemed shocking, at moments, that
> her mother who had been their source and centre was quite
> removed from their lives; it was nobody's fault (what be-
> comes of us, with all this living?) but Mother had irrevocably
> gone, and taken her ambience with her. Not only Mother had
> gone, but all those who . . . It is, she reflected, only the com-
> mon lot of ordinary people, of all of us, even the emperors,
> but something stays, added to the general sum, which is not

to connect this with the near-drowning of Ellen's nephew, the climax of Part III and indeed of the whole novel, there is an echo of the earlier drowning in the phrase used by the sailor-boy, "I sea-boy." (pp. 35, 176) Ellen's thought in Part I, that if she tells nobody about her mother's death it will not be real (p. 16) is echoed in Nora's similar thought about Johnny's deafness in Part III. (p. 146) The novel begins on the eve of Nora's wedding, and ends on the eve of Ellen's. At the beginning of the novel Ellen is convinced that Morgan Peake is not a fit husband for her sister; at the end, Ellen chooses Morgan to accompany her to the station to meet her own fiancé because in the intervening decade she has come to recognize Morgan's worth. Such devices do something to bind the parts of the novel together, but they fall well short of the effectiveness of such thematic motifs in *Swamp Angel* as the revolver itself and the migrating birds and swimming fish.

It is really Part II of the novel which defeats Mrs. Wilson's attempts to make this story a fully integrated one. She seems to have been conscious of this difficulty herself, for at the end of Part I she puts this passage, which seems to be an *apologia* for the inadequacy of Part II:

> In her much later life the long period which elapsed between the voyage and the meeting with her husband at the railway station seemed—erroneously—to Ellen to have passed with the fluidity and the sometimes violence of dreams, and therefore to be of no true significance. It is a fact that to one person a voyage may mean only a departure and an arrival, an expense incurred, only a happy lapse of coloured time, only an embarking and a disembarking— the distance between two places on a map which may be pink or even blue; but to Ellen the voyage was a shaking and transforming experience with which nothing in her future personal life was comparable, not even the events of the war because she was only one of millions of participants, and certainly not the years during which she worked for old Mr. Platt in Saskatoon—until she met George on the railway platform, and for the duration of her life thereafter. There is a curious semblance of reality in those of our years which are certainly valid, but seem to slide, and differ from our years of

reality. During those years of elision we live, of course, with relative intensity, and those years mark, retard, hasten, improve, or worsen us, and, alas, may affect some of those with whom we come into touch to a degree of pleasure, exasperation or even of damage, of which we are only partly aware; but then the true years of our life arrive—or do not arrive—and we forget those other irrelevant years which may, since Time is an agent, some day stir, and take their unexpected vengeance in a variety of ingenious ways. Such, at least, was Ellen's experience. (pp. 60–61)

There is a certain lameness about that passage, and its involved style reflects an inner uncertainty on its author's part. The thought is muddled, and the reference to Time taking its vengeance is a puzzling one which nothing in the remainder of the novel, so far as I can see, succeeds in clarifying. At the very least, this passage is an artistic blunder, since it tells us in advance that nothing of significance comparable to the voyage is to happen to Ellen until the meeting with George, which occurs on the very last pages of the novel. The whole of Part II, and much of Part III, have thus been dismissed in advance.

I suspect that passage of being a belated—and in my view misguided—interpolation. There are other hints that this novel was several times reworked by its author in an attempt to remedy its deficiencies. The opening pages of Part III, for example, by giving the full names of Ellen and Nora and by recapitulating other information already known to readers of Parts I and II, suggest that at one time this was intended as the beginning of an independent *novella*. And the sudden intrusion and quick disappearance of Merri Thompson on pages 152-53, and the reference to a "last time," suggest that there was at one time a scene introducing Merri which was subsequently deleted.

These, however, are relatively minor matters. The chief ways in which *Love and Salt Water* falls short of its predecessors are its thematic uncertainty and its relative paucity of unifying images and symbols.

III   *The Major Theme*

I believe that there is a single over-riding theme in *Love and Salt Water*, but it is far less clearly articulated than are the themes

just memory, and it does not do to mind . . . but she was
grateful to Nicola. (pp. 89-90)

In contrast, the marriage between George Gordon and his first
wife, Maidie, is no comfort at all, once the novelty of physical
intimacy has worn off:

> He and Maidie had lived together in short intervals of the
> war and in the years following the war. They had slept to-
> gether and woken together night after night and morning
> after morning—all the intimacy of marriage, and then came
> the niggling dissensions, the boredom, the deceptions of the
> enraging Maidie, the discoveries, the infidelity and Maidie
> shockingly up to her tricks and there was no more cajoling
> that had been so pretty and then so silly, and then so irri-
> tating. (pp. 92-93)

And so George is driven into solitude, from which he is to be
rescued by his projected marriage to Ellen. The gradual growth
of the love between Ellen and George, recurring at intervals
throughout the second half of the novel, is one of the most subtle
and sensitive elements in it. From a simple desire for companionship on the part of two bored and lonely people, it grows to a
passion strong enough to triumph over the tragic disfigurement
of Ellen's face. The novel ends with the prophecy of "their happy,
chequered life together." (p. 203)

Next in importance in the novel to the love between man and
woman is the love between parents and children. As always in
Mrs. Wilson's work, there is a strong sense of the family as a
bulwark against loneliness and the indifference of Time and
Nature. The love between Ellen and her parents, between Ellen
and her sister Nora, and between Ellen and her nephew Johnny,
is rich and fulfilling. But even the love of parent for child can
be excessive and unduly possessive. Nora's love for Johnny is of
this sort: "no woman should dare to be absorbed in her child as
Nora was absorbed in her son." (p. 66) Huw Peake, with whom
Ellen has a brief love affair in Part II, also has a possessive
mother: "She too often took the whips of love to him." (p. 73)
Indeed, love is not necessarily good: as Ellen realizes, if it is too
demanding it can become an "encroachment" against which we
must fortify ourselves. (p. 82)

Another equation of love is that between friends. Ellen thinks
of her relationship with Isa and Charles Cheney:

> This was a friendship, not of propinquity or convention, but
> of communication and love. Between Isa and Charles Cheney,
> and Gypsy Cuppy, and one or two more people whom she
> knew there was nothing which prevented communication
> or the unsaid word—nothing between. Their friendship was
> as clear as glass, as water, and as natural and refreshing as
> water. (p. 132)

This sense of solidarity can be achieved in special circumstances
even among people who do not know each other well. The passengers and crew in the great storm which is the climax of Part I
have this sense of unity. As the Dutch sailors sing and play, "bent
like lovers to their instruments" (p. 40) the whole scene takes
on symbolic overtones and we seem to be witnessing human
solidarity defying the hostile element of salt water to do its
worst:

> The sailors sang song after song, verse after verse, like
> hymns. There was the strange feeling of this room, this cave
> in the ocean full of sound, the sea beating on the ship, and
> the great dark unknown fish around and beneath the ship. . . .
> The bosun's boy gazed in wonder at the singing sailors and
> at the Christmas tree and at the passengers in their rather
> evening dress. His eyes shone wide like a child's shining eyes
> and were open. This is wonderful, thought Susan's daughter,
> I never in all my life saw anything like this—all these boys
> singing and the sea rushing. . . . (pp. 41-42)

Love then, in its various forms, is the chief—but not always an
adequate—bulwark against the destructive element, symbolized
by the sea or salt water. The same thought is conveyed by the
climactic scene in which Ellen's love for Johnny enables her to
save him from the great salt waves thrown up by the passing
ferry. Life is a stormy passage made tolerable by love; men,
living always "on a brink," (p. 192) must band together for mutual
comfort and solace. The natural universe is at worst hostile, at
best indifferent. There is a God to whom we may pray, but the
chief function of prayer is to make us aware of our membership
in the family of man. Susan tells Ellen (whose nickname is

Gypsy) that "Praying won't always take trouble away but it makes it easier for you and me to understand and manage:"

> "Prayer's like a cup, Gypsy, sent full of blessings from God."
> "The King doesn't have troubles, though?"
> "Yes, he does, God save him, because he's a man as well as a King. He has both kinds."
> "And does he have to pray, too?"
> "Yes, I think he prays every day and that helps him to be a good man, and you see, Gypsy, it makes us all one family. The prayer doesn't say 'Give *me* this day *my* daily bread,' it says 'Give *us our* daily bread' . . . and that means all of us."
> (p. 104)

There is no doubt that the need for people to band together in love is the dominant theme of the novel; but in her anxiety to be completely truthful, Mrs. Wilson has introduced so many minor qualifications into this main argument that the novel becomes almost unbearably complex. Love is basically good, but it is vulnerable to many abuses and subject to many limitations. There is the comfort of love—but there are the whips of love, the encroachments of love, and the excesses of love. Communication between people is good, but we "have to have reticences." (p. 149) "If you are happy and in love, no drive is dreary," (p. 74) but "Love (which is said to be enough) would not be enough." (p. 80) Sometimes, paradoxically, the gap between human beings closes when we recognize that the gap must exist. Ellen's meddling in Nora's relationship with Johnny nearly led to the boy's death, and Ellen reflects:

> She had better mind her own business. Everyone had better mind their own business. A gap had closed. (p. 188)

The attitude to love expressed there is similar to that of D. H. Lawrence, who sees love as the recognition of dynamic polarity rather than the urge to intimacy.

Just as love is treated with deliberate ambiguity, so is the sea and salt water. Basically, as we have seen, the sea is the destructive element, which drowns the innocent sailor boy and nearly drowns the seven-year-old Johnny. In the two sequences referred to, the sea's malignancy is emphasized: it is "of a curious lion colour, not to be trusted," (p. 43) an "irresistible force . . .

irresponsible . . ." "Like tigers at a safe distance," (p. 43) it "assailed the ship," (p. 44) "assaulted the ship," (p. 45) and was "a mad ocean" (p. 47) attacking the ship; while to Ellen in the rowboat with Johnny it is "a powerful tide" from which "there was no escaping." (p. 175) Elsewhere, however, the sea is pictured as something good, something to long for. In Saskatoon, "Ellen missed the salt water" (p. 83) and she decides that to escape boredom she must go "to the sea again." (p. 102) The Saviour-like Aunt Maury is described affectionately as having salt water in her veins. (p. 169) When Frank Cuppy is at his lowest point of loneliness, life appears to him as "a stale ditch," (p. 23) which implies that in contrast the salt water is fresh and invigorating. The resolution of the paradox seems to be that although the sea is the destructive element, it is also the element on which we can travel, the medium whereby we may give our lives dignity and meaning. Life lived on the brink is dangerous, but also exhilarating.

Ships, sea-birds, and sea-animals are the things which above all exhibit this capacity to use the sea creatively, and it is significant that references to these things dominate the imagery and symbolism of the novel. Ellen had a strong affinity for freighters and for tugs, "ordinary ships moving upon the water," (p. 7) and there are several eloquent descriptions of their grace and durability: they ride upon the sea, and they ride with style. So often does Ellen look with admiration and implied self-identification upon tugs, that we inevitably come to think of her as a kind of human tug, handsome, resolute, and proud:

> Out of the widening mouth of the creek came a medium-sized and handsome tug pulling two barges. Ellen detached herself from whatever it was that irritated her as she had stood in the room looking at her sister and her nephew, and became lost immediately in the extreme beauty of the tug and the way in which the tug rose and fell as it breasted and pushed forward against the running grey sea that opposed it.
>
> When Ellen visited her sister Nora Peake, she was sometimes disturbed in her thoughts. She even became bored and frequently turned her attention to the tugs that ply up and down the channel of False Creek. Each tug, large or small, high at the bow, low at the stern, has a proud bearing, and

has, indeed, a noble line and small dignity possessed by no other ship afloat. The tugs in this creek do not fuss around the high walls of large vessels, pushing and pulling; they proceed with gallant bearing up or down the channel, beginning or ending the tow's journey, or going on the way up the coast perhaps or to Vancouver Island, on the errand of picking up another tow and pulling it across the Gulf of Georgia in face of whatever weather there may be. There is, Ellen thought, something corporate about a tug when looked at from this height and distance. There were men, of course, on this small boat which she watched rising and dipping, with the seas parting white at its mouth and the two empty scows following biddably behind; but one could also imagine the tug itself as sentient, and, of itself, choosing and functioning. The tug bowed and rose and bowed again. (pp. 117-18)

Seagulls, herons, ducks, and especially cormorants also occur on a number of occasions, and again there is an element of self-identification on Ellen's part. The cormorant is ordinarily a symbol of greed and voraciousness, but for Ellen it seems to be a symbol of humility, courage, and tenacity:

On the base of Pompey's statua a cormorant sat. Its neck was long, a twisted periscope, a snake. She watched the black flight of another cormorant which settled on the low base of the statua, rose up, spread heraldic wings, subsided again, and spread the wings again, holding them for some time outspread and motionless. She thought about cormorants (strange birds); they are ugly and they are peculiarly beautiful . . . they sit without speaking, unlike gulls . . . do cormorants utter a word? . . . do they walk? . . . they do not sit on the top of the pillar as gulls do, but always low, on the base . . . why do they spread their wings like that, look, again . . . I once counted forty-five . . . she continued to herself. (pp. 118-19)

Ducks, on the other hand, are used to symbolize the endless cycle of life, to suggest the fundamental unity of all things:

Hundreds of small nameless ducks flowed slowly together in procession on the outgoing tide, replete after a morning's diving and feeding; they flowed and, suddenly, informed with one spirit of motion they all turned sharply against the tide (why? who conferred?), each with its sparkling riffle behind it, making a dazzle of water, and proceeded vigorously upstream in one long line, mysteriously deploying as one against the current, by-passing some mallards, by-passing a cormorant; the mallards, indifferent to the long line of little ducks with their wake of following glitter, came ashore, waddled with clumsy majesty and settled down to sleep instantly on the green grass; the very large cormorant, standing alone on a deadhead, extended its wings and held them motionless, heraldic; tugs issued from False Creek, and . . . if I live to be two hundred, thought Ellen, looking down from the balcony, exulting, I shall never tire of these water matters, seen from this nearness and height; it's life, and more than ordinary life and motion; I cannot explain it because I am not bird or water.

The simple scene conveyed to her that although by her humanity she was excluded, she was a part of these things. (pp. 129-30)

Recurrent references to dolphins, porpoises, turtles, and seals also suggest the possibility of survival in the sea: these creatures make of the destructive element a playground.

IV   *Subsidiary Themes*

Lively scenes involving animals or birds, usually with symbolic overtones, are a pervasive feature of Mrs. Wilson's fiction; a more unusual feature of this novel is the large part played in it by literary allusions. We have already noticed the implicit allusion to Arnold's "To Marguerite". On the very first page of the novel there is an obvious echo of Keats' "Ode on a Grecian Urn"; later on there are allusions to Marvell's "Coy Mistress," (p. 21) to Joyce Kilmer's "Trees," (p. 39) to *Hamlet*, (p. 78) to *The Notebooks of Samuel Butler*, (pp. 106 ff) to *Julius Caesar* (p. 118) and to Donne's "The Good-Morrow." (p. 155) Each of these allusions is used very cunningly to reinforce the themes of the novel. The excerpts from Butler's *Notebooks* all deal with various ways in which people estrange themselves from one another, or are estranged from life; Donne's poem celebrates the sense of magical freshness and communion which comes from true love; the allusion to *Hamlet* suggests the indecisiveness and inexplicable fits of temper which destroy Ellen's love for Huw Peake: thus these three allusions reinforce the main theme of the novel, that of love and loneliness. The Kilmer allusion is merely playful, but the allusions to Keats, Marvell and *Julius Caesar* reinforce the secondary theme of the novel: the vulnerability of human life, the inexorability of time, and the efforts of man through art, love and fame to escape the destructive wheels of "Time's winged chariot."

A more customary feature of Mrs. Wilson's art, also found in *Love and Salt Water,* is the symbolic use of light and darkness. Effects of light and darkness appear on almost every page, but the most conspicuous and sustained example occurs in Chapter XVIII. Almost the whole of that chapter is employed to bring out the idea that "perhaps our whole existence, one with another, is a trick of light." (p. 71) The rhythmic interplay of light and darkness is also invoked in Chapter XXXV, when Ellen has taken Johnny on the nearly fatal visit to Aunt Maury's summer cottage on Galiano Island:

> Since the cove at Uncle Dick and Aunt Maury's cottage faces west they see the beginning, the whole, and the last of the sunset. Every summer, as night comes on, the collection of visitors— one, two, ten—sprawl or sit on the dry moss, and, looking through the arbutus tree, watch the sky go wild. Aunt Maury thought and spoke on one such night in that very summer that Ellen took Johnny there, of the "Amen" at the end of Rossini's Stabat Mater. There was the first melodious affirmation, darkening clouds in the sky; then there was the glory from horizon to zenith; then came the solemn affirmation, the final statement "Amen, Amen, this day is done," and there was night. (pp. 158-59)

There is also found in this novel, though rather less prominently than usual, Mrs. Wilson's fascination with "innocence." Once more we find her using the words "innocent" and "innocence" with a special meaning. Why, for example, is the death of Ellen's mother described as "innocent?" (p. 20) Presumably because it is natural, part of a cycle that we should accept. Why is Ellen, watching the

new love grow up between her father and Nicola Gracey, "caught
on a margin of innocence and surprise?" (pp. 53-54) Because,
I take it, she is, at sixteen, too old to accept the naturalness of
such a love, as would a child, and too young to be shocked at
such a sudden transfer of affection, as adults would be. Mr. and
Mrs. Ransome, who bore Ellen and Huw Peake when they visit
them, "are innocent and tiresome and quite old" (p. 79)—innocent, again, in the sense that their state is perfectly natural, their
tiresomeness (to the young), the spontaneous expression of their
age. Mountain streams are "innocent" (p. 150) because in rushing down the hillsides they are doing what it is in their nature
to do. But Ethel Wilson is not naive nor sentimental; she does not
suggest that innocence is an armour. The sea-boy and Johnny are
"innocents," but one is drowned and the other nearly so. Innocence is attractive to Mrs. Wilson, but she is under no illusions
about its invulnerability.

Another common feature in Mrs. Wilson's work that recurs
in *Love and Salt Water* is her love for British Columbia in particular and Canada in general. In Chapter XXIV especially she
pays her tribute to her adopted country. Here are one or two
samples:

> No picture can show how wide the country is; no map convey.
> Once traversing will not do. Each time the uninterested
> traveller crosses the Dominion of Canada by the northern
> route, by the southern route, or by air, the journey becomes
> more intolerably long, the forests more intolerably endless,
> the prairies are more boringly monotonous, the lakes inter-
> minable, the mountains monstrous, until the Pacific Ocean
> is reached. Each time the interested traveller crosses the
> country by the northern route, by the southern route or by
> air, the country with its sleeping past, its awakened future,
> the gradual progress of discovery and habitation, the extrava-
> gant forests, prairies, lakes, and mountains, the great beauty,
> the isolated and sometimes collapsed shack that speaks of
> human effort and departure, the sudden appearance of a
> city in all that solitude (like an explosion)—the land enchants
> and speaks to him. The land is full of question. The journey
> disturbs and exhilarates. (pp. 96-97)

> The formidable power of geography determines the char-
> acter and performance of a people; it invokes understanding

or prejudice; it makes peace or war. A land that stretches across a continent extends in breadth and in some homogeneity; it gives flattering promise of peace; but in a land which is crushed in the middle of Europe or Asia, anxieties are renewed. It is the fault of geography. (p. 99)

V *Style and Tone*

Above all, *Love and Salt Water* exhibits Mrs. Wilson's usual skill as a stylist. The tone throughout is beautifully modulated—from irony to sentiment, from poetic suggestion to prosaic statement, from witty aside to solemn affirmation. The words and phrases seldom draw attention to themselves, but when we stop to examine them we are always struck by their exactness of denotation and their aptness of connotation. Metaphors and similes are almost as frequent in her prose as in most poetry, but they never scintillate with a useless brilliance—they always echo or reinforce theme.

Thus *Love and Salt Water*, although it lacks that final unity of effect which so distinguishes the best of Mrs. Wilson's work in fiction, is a novel of unusual subtlety and delicacy. At each reading it challenges one anew by its elusive and allusive suggestions of the human quest for love and permanence among the shifting waves of the salt, estranging sea.

CHAPTER 8

Conclusion

I STATED in the introduction to this study that it is difficult to categorize the fiction of Ethel Wilson, and I hope that my examination of her work has revealed the source of this difficulty. Each of her novels is such a highly integrated work of art that it is impossible to say whether it is primarily a novel of manners, of theme, or of character. The development of society described so skillfully in *The Innocent Traveller*, for example, cannot be isolated from the development of the character of Aunt Topaz, any more than Aunt Topaz' character can be isolated from the main theme of innocence and experience, time and eternity. Similarly, it is impossible to say whether Lilly, in *Lilly's Story*, carries the theme of that novella, or whether the theme carries Lilly: one simply cannot think of one without thinking of the other. It is this ability to weave all elements of the art of fiction into a single fabric that is Ethel Wilson's highest distinction. She has a shrewd insight into social behaviour and individual character, a strong sense of place and abundant gifts for description, a wise and balanced view of man and his relationship to the universe, an eye for the revealing symbol or image, and a clear, simple and yet almost unerringly deft style; but each of these capacities is employed to reinforce the others.

As a social chronicler, Mrs. Wilson charms us by her wit and by her effortless attention to the minutiae of daily life. To her, social relationships and arrangements are a kind of game, to be observed with ironic detachment. The flush toilet appears in the opening pages of *The Innocent Traveller* as a new kind of toy; Aunt Topaz' bicycle is another toy. Changes in the means of transport, of entertainment, or of communication are all unobtrusively recorded in her novels, and they help to give us that sense of the continuous flow of time which is one of the strengths of her work. But there is nothing portentous about her social documentation, none of Zola's heavy-handed historicity. This lightness of touch, this detachment of attitude, is part of Ethel Wilson's wisdom: life becomes tolerable if we refuse to take its trivia too seriously. The comic spirit is an essential part of her art. Like Housman, she sees that in a limited sense at least "the feather-pate of folly / Bears the falling sky."

The comic spirit also plays a large part in her characterization of individuals. Aunt Topaz, the Reverend Elmer Pratt, Yow, Myrt and Mort, Mrs. Emblem and Mrs. Severance are all creations of the comic spirit, "characters" as well as characters, eccentrics who are cherished as samples of the immense variety of human behaviour. But here as elsewhere Mrs. Wilson is a very balanced writer. There is a serious, almost a tragic, dimension even to these more lightly presented characters: even the ebullient and volatile Aunt Topaz must eventually become a victim of senility and death; Yow becomes a thief and a bully; Mort dies a death that is at least to some degree tragic; Mrs. Severance has to give up her beloved revolver and with it her attachment to a romantic past. And there are, of course, other characters in whom the tragic element dominates: Victoria May Tritt, for example, the lonely spinster in *Tuesday and Wednesday,* or the unhappy Vera Gunnarsen in *Swamp Angel.*

Perhaps the most remarkable thing about Mrs. Wilson's characterization is the way in which it observes her own principle of simultaneous involvement and detachment. Never is a character held up merely to ridicule on the one hand, or merely to sympathy on the other. Mrs. Wilson sees into and through and around her characters. Admirable as is Aunt Topaz, she is seen to be full of faults; heroic as is Lilly, she is mean, devious and selfish almost to the last. This again is part of Mrs. Wilson's wisdom: she takes people as she finds them, is neither unduly idealistic nor unduly cynical about human behaviour.

Another strong point of her characterization is the development which occurs in almost all of her characters. Frankie, in *Hetty Dorval,* develops from a naive country girl to a mature and sophisticated young woman; Lilly, in *Lilly's Story,* from a weak, irresponsible flirt to a deeply serious and almost selfless mother and wife; and each novel provides additional examples. The development is almost always in the direction of greater wisdom, tolerance and understanding: life, for Mrs. Wilson as for E. M. Forster, is largely a matter of development of the undeveloped heart. In almost all her novels, her chief protagonists confront a crisis or series of crises which shock them out of their complacent egoism into some kind of self-surrender or self-transcendence.

The sane and balanced but very sensitive portrayal of human character extends also to Ethel Wilson's treatment of the physical environment. By her detailed but never exhausting descriptions of the rivers and mountains and lush valleys of British Columbia, of the mountains and water that surround Vancouver, of Vancouver's streets and houses and public buildings, and of such conspicuous features of the Canadian landscape as the lonely prairies and the brilliance of the Northern Lights, she makes clear her affection for and delight in these places and phenomena. But she never ignores their harsher, more forbidding aspects. The Thompson River, in *Hetty Dorval*, is seen as beautiful but also as fiercely destructive; often the salt water off the British Columbia coast destroys those of her characters who sail upon it; the streets and houses of Vancouver are often seen as mean and shoddy; the Northern Lights spell not only beauty but an immense and frightening indifference to human aspiration.

A similarly balanced treatment is accorded to the birds and animals which share man's physical habitation. It is obvious that Mrs. Wilson loves birds and animals, so closely does she observe and record their behaviour, but she shows herself aware also of their capacity for cruelty and greed. Even a kitten, as we see in *Lilly's Story*, can change in an instant from a cuddly plaything into a beast of prey.

But it is perhaps in relating man to his inanimate and animate environment that Mrs. Wilson shows her greatest skill. She perceives the fundamental unity of all things, what Mrs. Severance calls "the everlasting web." There is a cosmic rhythm, and true life consists in surrendering oneself to that rhythm. If man seeks to preserve his own personal identity, to protect himself within the shell of his own ego, he brings upon himself loneliness, fear, and ultimate horror.

Here we must invoke one of Mrs. Wilson's favourite words, the word which is perhaps the chief clue to her unique vision of life, "innocence." Over and over again this word, or its adjective "innocent," is used in her novels and stories, often in a most surprising context. Topaz as a small child is "as innocent as a poached egg"; the Reverend Elmer Pratt greets his parishioners "with innocent ghoulish pleasure"; the day that Mrs. Hamilton Coffin takes swimming lessons from Joe Fortes is "an innocent blue day"; Aunt Topaz for all her faults is an "innocent traveller"; when Lilly arrives at Comox she wears her "innocent black," and when she is lying to Mrs. Butler about her family she looks at her "with the full impact of her innocence"; the kitten is described as innocent the very moment before he attacks the robin; the confrontation, in *Swamp Angel,* of a fawn and a kitten is described as "a sight of perfect innocence"; the death of Ellen's mother, in *Love and Salt Water,* is described as innocent, and Ellen, seeing her father fall in love with a second woman, is "caught on a margin of innocence and surprise"; Mr. and Mrs. Ransome, an old couple in that novel, are "innocent and tiresome and quite old," and mountain streams rushing downhill are also innocent.

Innocence for Mrs. Wilson obviously has a meaning much broader than guiltlessness, naiveté, ignorance or inexperience: it is used rather in the sense that Blake used it, as a recognition that "all that lives is holy." Innocence for her seems to sum up all the virtues, to include a recognition of the sacredness of one's own nature, of the sacredness of the nature of others, and of the sacredness of the physical environment. Aunt Topaz, for all her faults, is an innocent because she fulfills her own personality but never interferes in the fulfillment of others; Lilly is an innocent because, in spite of much deviousness, she fulfills her role as a mother and, eventually, as a wife; the kitten is an innocent because it obeys the instincts of its own nature; Mrs. Severance becomes an innocent when she releases her selfish grip on her own romantic past; Vera Gunnarsen will probably never become innocent because she cannot break out of the circle of her own egoism. Innocence is a commitment to life, movement, growth, activity; it can even, when time is ripe, be a commitment to death. It is a giving, a surrender, but at the same time a fulfillment and an enhancement of one's own being.

The use which Mrs. Wilson makes of this ambiguous concept of innocence suggests that for all her good sense and ironic detachment there is a mystical quality in her work. She sees man and his universe as involved in a rhythmic pulsation between polarities: innocence and experience, responsibility and irresponsibility, unity and diversity, love and loneliness, faith and fear, glory and horror, time and timelessness. Man himself is a tissue of contrarieties: he is fragile but tenacious, fond of solitude and yet afraid of loneliness. The creatures of the animal kingdom are likewise divided beings, friendly and yet fierce, beautiful but cruel. Nature delights man by its beauty, but in flood or storm it destroys him. Man's role, as a fragile creature in a world which has other ends than his comfort, is a difficult but supportable one. He must be alert, as were Lilly and Maggie, to his own interests, and yet not obsessed by them, as was Vera Gunnarsen; he must preserve his own identity and yet be willing to merge it in the comforting community of a marriage; the family community can also support him, but if he allows it to dominate him it can destroy his individuality; he must beware that man is not an island entire unto itself and thus recognize the fundamental unity of all mankind, and yet he must respect the sacredness of his own unique personality and accept the fact that in the final analysis each of us is alone.

But all this suggests that Mrs. Wilson's novels are far more abstract and didactic than they really are. All that she writes does spring from a vision of reality similar to that which I have just inexpertly outlined, but her views are never obtrusive or simplistic. This is because her themes are suggested rather than stated, conveyed through character and event rather than by abstract moralizing. They are also projected, but always cunningly, through the use of symbols and thematic images. The sea-gulls in the latter pages of *The Innocent Traveller*, for example, convey to us subtly but clearly Mrs. Wilson's sense of the mingled beauty and ferocity of the animal kingdom; and the various water images in that novel convey to us her sense of the continuous ebb and flow of time. *Swamp Angel*, as we have seen, is dominated throughout by images of flight and flow; and indeed each of her novels, and most of her short stories, has a dominant thematic image or symbol which at once suggests the novel's meaning and gives it aesthetic coherence.

Of Mrs. Wilson's style in the narrower sense of the choice and arrangement of words into sentences and paragraphs, it is perhaps enough to state that she lives up to her own preference as expressed in the following portion of a letter to me, dated July 12, 1953:

> If you ask me to look at what I most like—I like the English sentence, clear, un-lush, and un-loaded. . . . It is like architecture; it should have a function and be very beautiful. Ornament it if you really wish; or perhaps it flows into ornament naturally. But I like the formal and simple sentence best.

There is no rhetorical splendour in her writing, no unfunctional ornament, and no unnecessary complexity. Her words are colloquial, casual, mainly monosyllabic, and they are arranged into mainly short, declarative sentences. She never seeks to dazzle us, but merely to enlighten.

Of style in the larger sense—the disposition and arrangement of material, the creation and maintenance of atmosphere and mood, the management of tone—Mrs. Wilson is equally an undemonstrative master. She writes almost always with great tact, with unspectacular skill. When she wishes, as in *Hetty Dorval,* she can put together an intricate plot with great cunning; usually she is content with the straightforward marshalling of scenes in chronological order. Only occasionally, as in the weak middle section of *Love and Salt Water,* does her skill falter. She creates and maintains atmosphere by accumulating precise touches of observation and description, by such sensuous particularity that we are never conscious, until we look for them, of the means by which the end has been achieved. Her management of tone is especially praiseworthy: gentle, casual, ironic, at once involved and detached, she presents us with the products of her observation and allows us to make our own judgments upon them. If she comments herself upon her observations, she almost always does so shyly and tentatively, as if inviting our concurrence or dissent. Sometimes there is a slightly irritating coyness or archness of tone—as in the references to Mort's "angel" in *Tuesday and Wednesday*—but these rare failures are only remembered because they are so rare.

Ethel Wilson lays no claim to being a major novelist, but she is a minor novelist of genuine distinction whose work will almost certainly be read when that of many more pretentious and prolific writers is forgotten. In the narrower context of the still emerging literature of Canada, she is a figure of great importance. She is one of the very few Canadian writers for whom one need make no apology in offering her work to the world. She belongs in the main tradition of the English novel, has her affiliations as we have seen with Defoe, Fielding, Trollope, Bennett and Forster, and yet she is unmistakably an artist of twentieth century Canada. She neither pleads for nor repudiates her own country, but writes of it with balance and dignity. She seeks to be neither fashionable nor defiantly unfashionable, but expresses her own vision honestly and in the form which suits it best. Self-consciousness, both in the personal and national sense, has perhaps been the chief bane of writing in Canada, situated as we are between the mellow traditions of the Old World and the aggressive experimentation of the New, and it is Mrs. Wilson's special legacy that her work is not self-conscious at all. Like the writers she most admires, she has a limpid style, lacks pretentiousness, has something to say, and says it with skill and with good heart. Like theirs, her work gives "inexpressible pleasure."

Notes and References

Chapter One

1. "A Cat Among the Falcons," *Canadian Literature*, II (Autumn, 1959), 16.
2. Letter, dated Vancouver, July 12 [1953].
3. Letter, dated Bowen Island, B.C., July 25 [1953].
4. "The Bridge or the Stokehold?" *Canadian Literature*, V (Summer, 1960), 46.
5. Mrs. Wilson later corrected "cynicism" to "scepticism," in a letter, dated Vancouver, July 15 [1953].
6. Letter, dated Bowen Island, B.C., July 25 [1953].
7. Letter, dated Vancouver, July 12 [1953].
8. Letter, dated Vancouver, July 15 [1953]. See also "Reflections in a Pool," *Canadian Literature*, XXII (Autumn, 1964), 30.
9. "Reflections in a Pool," p. 31.
10. *Ibid.*
11. Letter, dated Vancouver, July 12 [1953].
12. *Canadian Literature*, II (Autumn, 1959), 16–17.
13. Letter, dated Vancouver, July 12 [1953].
14. See "A Series of Combination of Events and Where is John Goodwin," *Tamarack Review*, XXXIII (Autumn, 1964), 3–9.
15. Letter, dated Vancouver, July 12 [1953].
16. *Canadian Literature*, II (Autumn, 1959), 12.
17. *Ibid.*, p. 13.
18. *Canadian Literature*, V (Summer, 1960), 47.
19. *Saturday Review of Literature*, Dec. 10, 1949, p. 17.
20. *Canadian Forum*, XXXII (August, 1952), 117.
21. *New York Times Book Review Section*, May 3, 1953, p. 5.
22. *Spectator*, Sept. 3, 1954, p. 294.
23. *Tamarack Review*, XXII (Winter, 1962), 95–96.
24. *Proceedings and Transactions of the Royal Society of Canada*, 4th Series, II (1964), 63–64.

Chapter Two

1. Ethel Wilson, *Mrs. Golightly and Other Stories* (Toronto: Macmillan, 1961), 209 pp.
    All subsequent page references in this chapter, unless otherwise identified, are to this edition of this book.
2. Letter, dated March 27 [1966].
3. *Journal of the Royal Architectural Institute of Canada*, April, 1959, p. 130.
4. *Tamarack Review*, I (Autumn, 1956), 7–17.
5. *Ibid.*, pp. 7–8.
6. *Canadian Literature*, I (Autumn, 1959), 10–19.
7. "To Keep the Memory of so Worthy a Friend," *Mrs. Golightly and Other Stories*, pp. 89–96.
8. *Canadian Literature*, XXII (Autumn, 1964), 29–33.
9. *Tamarack Review*, XXXIII (Autumn, 1964), 3–9.
10. *Canadian Literature*, XIX (Winter, 1964), 33–42.

Chapter Three

1. Ethel Wilson, *Hetty Dorval*, (Toronto: Macmillan, 1947), 116 pp.
    All subsequent page references in this chapter are to this edition of the novel.

Chapter Four

1. Ethel Wilson, *The Innocent Traveller*, (Toronto: Macmillan, 1949), 277 pp.
    All subsequent page references in this chapter are to this edition of the novel.

Chapter Five

1. Ethel Wilson, *The Equations of Love* (Toronto: Macmillan, 1952), 281 pp.
    All subsequent page references in this chapter are to this edition of the book.
2. *New Yorker*, XXIX (May 9, 1953), 137.

Chapter Six

1. Ethel Wilson, *Swamp Angel* (Toronto: Macmillan, 1954), 216 pp.
 All subsequent page references in this chapter are to this first Canadian edition of the novel. The American edition, published by Harper's, has two additional chapters (XII and XLIV) which give additional information about Vera Gunnarsen's early life.

Chapter Seven

1. Ethel Wilson, *Love and Salt Water,* (Toronto: Macmillan, 1956), 203 pp.
 All subsequent page references in this chapter are to this edition of the novel.

Selected Bibliography

PRIMARY SOURCES

I. *Books by Ethel Wilson:*
Hetty Dorval. Toronto and London: Macmillan, 1947.
The Innocent Traveller. Toronto and London: Macmillan, 1949.
The Equations of Love. Toronto and London: Macmillan, 1952.
    also: *Equazioni d'Amore.* Milan: Martello, 1958.
        Lilly; Roman. Zurich: Humanitas, 1952.
        Lilly's Story. New York: Harper, 1953.
        Lilly. Copenhagen: Samlerens, 1954.
Swamp Angel. Toronto and London: Macmillan, 1954.
    also: New York: Harper, 1954.
        Toronto: McClelland and Stewart, 1962.
Love and Salt Water. Toronto and London: Macmillan, 1956.
    also: New York: St. Martin's Press, 1957.
Mrs. Golightly and Other Stories. Toronto and London: Macmillan, 1961.

II. *Short Stories by Ethel Wilson:*
"I Just Love Dogs," *New Statesman and Nation,* XIV (December 4, 1937), 929–30.*
    (Reprinted in *Best British Short Stories of 1938,* ed. E. O'Brien. Boston: Houghton Mifflin, 1938.)
"Hurry, hurry!" *New Statesman and Nation,* XVIII (November 25, 1939), 754–55.*
    (Reprinted in *A Book of Canadian Short Stories,* ed. D. Pacey. Toronto: Ryerson, 1950.)
"On Nimpish Lake," *Canadian Forum,* XXII (July, 1942), 119–20.*
"We have to sit opposite," *Chatelaine,* (May, 1945), 15, 46–47.

"The Cigar and the Poor Young Girl," *Echoes* (Autumn, 1945), 11, 46.

"Mrs. Golightly and the First Convention," *Canadian Short Stories,* eds. R. Weaver and H. James. Toronto: 1952, 151–64.*

(Reprinted in *Cavalcade of the North,* ed. G. E. Nelson. Garden City, N.Y.: Doubleday, 1958.)

"The Birds," *Northern Review,* VII (October–November, 1954), 24–27.*

"The Window," *Tamarack Review,* VIII (Summer, 1958), 3–16.*

(Reprinted in *Best American Short Stories: 1959,* eds. M. Foley and D. Burnett. Boston: Houghton Mifflin, 1959.)

"A Drink With Adolphus," *Tamarack Review,* XVI (Summer, 1960), 5–16.*

"Simple Translation," *Saturday Night,* LXXVI (December 23, 1961), 19.

(Condensed version in *Reader's Digest* [April, 1962], under the title "Journey to a Fair Land.")

"A Visit to the Frontier," *Tamarack Review,* XXXIII (Autumn, 1964), 55–65.

* Denotes inclusion in *Mrs. Golightly and Other Stories.*

III. *Essays by Ethel Wilson:*

"On a Portuguese Balcony," *Tamarack Review,* I (Autumn, 1956), 7–17.

"To keep the memory of so worthy a friend," *Reporter,* XV (December 13, 1956), 35–36.*

"Address to the Students of the School of Architecture, U.B.C.," *Royal Architectural Institute of Canada Journal,* XXXVI (April, 1959), 130–33.

"A Cat Among the Falcons," *Canadian Literature,* II (Autumn, 1959), 10–19.

(Reprinted in *Masks of Fiction,* ed. A. J. M. Smith. Toronto: McClelland and Stewart, 1961.)

"The Bridge or the Stokehold?" *Canadian Literature,* V (Summer, 1960), 43–47.

"Of Alan Crawley," *Canadian Literature,* XIX (Winter, 1964), 32–42.

"Reflections in a Pool," *Canadian Literature,* XXII (Autumn, 1964), 29–33.

"A Series of Combination of Events & Where is John Goodwin," *Tamarack Review,* XXXIII (Autumn, 1964), 3–9.

* Denotes inclusion in *Mrs. Golightly and Other Stories.*

IV. *Excerpts from novels by Ethel Wilson:*

"I have a father in the Promised Land," (from *The Innocent Traveller*), *New Statesman and Nation,* XVII (February 4, 1939), 167–69.

"The Innumerable Laughter," (from *The Innocent Traveller*), *Orion,* IV (Autumn, 1947), 121–30.

"Down at English Bay," (from *The Innocent Traveller*), *Here and Now,* I (May, 1948), 7–12.

"The Funeral Home," (from *The Equations of Love*), *Northern Review,* IV (April–May, 1951), 12–15.

"Miss Tritt," (from *The Equations of Love*), *Northern Review,* V (October–November, 1951), 11–19.

(Reprinted in *Canadian Anthology,* eds. C. F. Klinck and R. E. Watters. Toronto: W. J. Gage, 1955.)

"The Escape," (from *Swamp Angel*), *Northern Review,* VI (June–July, 1953), 2–7.

untitled excerpt (from *Swamp Angel*), *Queen's Quarterly,* LX (Winter, 1954), 526–31.

SECONDARY SOURCES

I. *General criticism:*

Clarke, Mrs. Rita. "Appearance and Reality in the Fiction of Ethel Wilson" (thesis, University of British Columbia, 1964).

An attempt to isolate the major themes in the novels and stories.

Livesay, Dorothy. "Ethel Wilson: West Coast Novelist," *Saturday Night,* LXVII (July 26, 1952), 20, 36.

A biographical and critical sketch, written by one of Canada's leading poets.

Pacey, Desmond. "The Innocent Eye: The Art of Ethel Wilson," *Queen's Quarterly,* LXI (Spring, 1954), 45–52.

A general review of Ethel Wilson's first three novels,

finding their core in the concept of "innocence," in the
Blakeian sense of the unspoiled vision.

Sonthoff, H. W. "The Novels of Ethel Wilson," *Canadian
Literature*, XXVI (Autumn, 1965), 33–42.
This perceptive but brief article concentrates on the
modulation of tone in Mrs. Wilson's fiction.

Watters, R. E. "Ethel Wilson, The Experienced Traveller,"
B.C. Library Quarterly, XXI (April, 1958), 21–27.
This article provides a balance to Pacey's earlier one by
emphasising the maturity and depth of vision which
modifies Ethel Wilson's "innocence."

II. *Selected book reviews:*

Hetty Dorval
Culture, IX (June, 1948), 214–15.
N.Y. Herald Tribune Book Review (October 19, 1947),
14.
Times Literary Supplement (July 24, 1948), 413.
University of Toronto Quarterly, XVII (April, 1948),
272.

The Innocent Traveller
Canadian Forum, XXIX (December, 1949), 214.
N.Y. Herald Tribune Book Review (January 15, 1950), 6.
Saturday Night, LXV (October 11, 1949), 46.
Saturday Review, XXXII (December 10, 1949), 17.
University of Toronto Quarterly, XIX (April, 1950), 275.

The Equations of Love
Canadian Forum, XXXII (August, 1952), 117.
Northern Review, VI, no. 2 (June–July, 1953), 36–40.
Saturday Night, LXVII (April 5, 1952), 28.
Spectator, CLXXXVIII (March 21, 1952), 378.
Times Literary Supplement (March 28, 1952), 217.
University of Toronto Quarterly, XXII (April, 1953,
288–90, 292.

Lilly's Story (Harper, U.S.A.)
N.Y. Herald Tribune Book Review (May 3, 1953), 4.
New York Times Book Review Section (May 3, 1953), 5.
Saturday Review, XXXVI (May 16, 1953), 42.

Swamp Angel
Canadian Forum, XXXIV (February, 1955), 263.

N.Y. Herald Tribune Book Review (September 5, 1954), 4.

New York Times Book Review Section (August 29, 1954), 17.

Queen's Quarterly, LXI (Winter, 1955), 555–56.

Saturday Review, XXXVII (September 4, 1954), 22.

Spectator, CXCIII (September 3, 1954), 294.

Times Literary Supplement (August 27, 1954), 541.

Love and Salt Water

Queen's Quarterly, LXIV (Spring, 1957), 143–44.

Saturday Night, LXXI (November 24, 1956), 32.

Times Literary Supplement (October 5, 1956), 581.

Mrs. Golightly and Other Stories

Canadian Forum, XLI (March, 1962), 285.

Canadian Literature, XI (Winter, 1962), 67–68.

Queen's Quarterly, LXIX (Summer, 1962), 311.

Saturday Night, LXXVI (October 28, 1961), 41–42.

Tamarack Review, XXII (Winter, 1962), 95–96.

University of Toronto Quarterly, XXXI (July, 1962), 471–72.

Index